JANE AUSTEN
CELEBRATES

Holidays AND Occasions
Regency Style

LINDY BELL

Jane Austen Celebrates

Editor: Laura Bangarter

Print and eBook Interior Design: Dayna Linton, Day Agency

Library of Congress Control Number: Pending

Day Agency
South Jordan UT

ISBN 978-0-692-94526-1 Print Book
ISBN 978-0-692-94527-8 E-Book

First Edition: 2017

10 9 8 7 6 5 4 3 2 1

Printed in the USA

Dedication

For Mom and Dad

This book exists because of your love, support and never-tiring belief and encouragement.

From the bottom of my heart,
Thank You

JANE AUSTEN
CELEBRATES

Holidays AND Occasions
Regency Style

Foreword

———✦———

I T IS TWO SEPARATE things to be an admirer of and to be a big fan of Jane Austen. To be an admirer means to revere the genius of her writing. Her keen observation of and depiction of human nature has resonated with readers for over 200 years along with her skillful manipulation of intricate plots that result in the ultimate happy resolution. To be a fan, means to enjoy and revel in all things related not just to her writing but to her life and her times as well. I would term myself both a Jane Austen admirer and fan.

Through research for this book, I have enjoyed the opportunity to delve deeper into Jane Austen's life, the times in which she lived, her personal letters and her novels. It has been an interesting journey to gain an even deeper understanding of this amazing author while discovering how she and her fellow Regency Era dwellers celebrated holidays and occasions. You might just be surprised at many familiar customs we still celebrate today.

I hope you enjoy . . .

A Regency Holiday Journey Begins

"I tell you all the Good I can, as I know how much you will enjoy it."
Jane Austen in a letter to her sister, Cassandra ~ March 1814

A YEAR FULL OF REGENCY Era celebrations lies before us. Let's explore how much we have in common with Jane Austen and her fellow Regency Era dwellers in celebrating holidays and sharing special times with family and friends.

Officially, the Regency Era covered the nine years between February of 1811 and January of 1820. In 1810, reigning King George III, famously known as the British monarch who ruled during the American Revolution, became seriously ill. He was so ill in fact, he could no longer rule due to mental incapacity. As a result, in 1811, the Regency Act was passed placing his son, George, on the throne as Prince Regent. Prince George ruled until his father's death in 1820. At that time, he ascended the throne as King George IV and ruled in his own right.

The short duration of the Regency period, only nine years, had far-reaching and long-lasting effects. What generated such interest and devotion in these nine years? Why did it give rise to so many romantic novels featuring lovely heroines and dashing heroes living in refined elegance and attuned to fine manners and high fashion? Perhaps the answer lies in the Prince Regent himself for whom the

time period gets its name. The Prince was the epitome of London's idealization of elegance, etiquette and romance immediately prior to and even after his assuming the throne. Young George was handsome, charming, extravagant, a prince and darling of the London set. This flamboyant image has firmly established the Prince as the embodiment of the Regency Era and has forever linked him to the genteel times integral to the novels of Jane Austen.

The Prince Regent
The Jane Austen Center

During the Prince's height of popularity, society in Regency England flourished with an abundance of balls and soirees; shooting and hunting parties, tea parties and fox hunts. Beyond all the gaiety of these social events, how did period dwellers live day-to-day and most particularly, how did they celebrate holidays and special occasions? Let's take a stroll through a typical Regency year and discover the holidays they celebrated and customs associated with each. We might even recognize some traditions as they have evolved through the years into ways we celebrate today.

So off we go. Tie on your bonnet, don your pelisse and step into the courtyard for a Regency year full of fun, surprises and happy times shared with friends and family.

January

A Great Beginning & Even Better Ending

"I have now attained the true art of letter-writing, which we are always told, is to express on paper exactly what one would say to the same person by word of mouth; I have been talking to you almost as fast as I could the whole of this letter."
Jane Austen in a letter to her sister, Cassandra ~ January 1801

IT MIGHT SEEM THAT January has always been the first month of the year and January 1st has always been New Year's Day. Interestingly, though, that wasn't the case until 1752. Prior to 1752, March 25th, also known as Lady Day, was recognized as the first of the new year since it came at the first of spring.

Prior to and into the early 1800s, calendars were not readily available so the changing of the seasons was the most effective and easiest way to mark holidays. March 25th came at the beginning of spring and with the earth coming to life again, it all correlated to new life and new beginnings which included the start of a new year.

The first of the new year changed when the British government adopted the Gregorian calendar in 1752 and January became the beginning of the year. By the time of the Regency Era, this change was still rather new so Regency Era dwellers were in the process of adapting to the

new year coming in the middle of winter.

While the cold, snowy month of January might seem a bit dreary, the holidays celebrated in this month are actually a joyous part of the Yuletide season associated with Christmas and Boxing Day. The twelve-day period between Christmas and Twelfth Night is filled with balls, parties and age-old traditions. Let's skip ahead for now and start in February. We'll anticipate celebrating the Yuletide holidays of Epiphany and Twelfth Night when we circle back to January amid celebrations of the Christmastide season in December.

On we go! Let's journey ahead and see what February holds in store.

February

❧❦❧

A Month to Warm One's Heart

'A farmer should, on Candlemas Day,
Have half his corn and half his hay.'
'On Candlemas Day if the thorns hang adrop,
You can be sure of a good pea crop.'

Farmer's Candlemas Proverb

CANDLEMAS - CANDLES & LIGHT

ANDLEMAS, THE FIRST LOVELY holiday in February, is celebrated between the December solstice and the March equinox. Many traditionally considered this time of year as the midpoint of winter between the shortest day of the year and the spring equinox. Candlemas was typically observed on February 2nd and today, is observed as a Christian holiday. There is some debate whether Candlemas evolved from the pagan Gaelic festival known as *Imbolc*. The word *Imbolc* means "ewe-milk." Since lambs were born at this time of year in old England and brought with them the flow of their mother's ewe milk, the season was named in its recognition. The goddess, *Imbolc*, was said to have used candles to banish dark spirits. The Romans also observed the tradition of lighting candles to chase away evil spirits during the dark days of winter. Candlemas was also known as the 'Feast of Lights' and celebrated the

increasing warmth of the life-giving sun as winter made its way into spring.

The Christian observance of Candlemas celebrates Mary's presentation of the baby Jesus in the temple. The February 2nd date of observance marks the 40th day following the December 25th celebrated birth of Christ. In the New Testament, the Bible says in Luke 2:25-33 that a Jewish man by the name of Simeon, moved by the Holy Spirit, went into the temple courts. When he held baby Jesus in his arms, Simeon declared the babe would be *a light* to the world. Christians consider Jesus to be the light of the world so for this reason, the holiday is called Candlemas and celebrated with the lighting of candles.

Some Christians began celebrating Candlemas in Jerusalem as early as the fourth century and began celebrating the holiday with the lighting of candles in the fifth century. Other sources say the holiday was celebrated by lighting candles as far back as the 11th century. Candles, as a source of light, were an important part of everyday and were believed at one time to be a protection against plague and famine. It was a day when candles were traditionally brought into the church and blessed and a candlelit procession held in observance. The celebrations came together to become a festival day or "mass" of the candles.

Brigit, the goddess of spring, was celebrated at a feast on February 2nd. Brigit was thought be a "diviner" or "able to see into the future" and eventually became the patron saint of weather forecasters. Fittingly, Candlemas Day across Europe was considered to be an especially good day for predicting the weather for the year to come. Some

thought lovely weather on Candlemas Day meant that winter would continue for another 40 days while storms and clouds meant warm weather and spring were soon to arrive. This custom is still familiar to us today as Groundhog Day. Weather proverbs were even written in celebration of the tradition.

Candlemas Weather Proverb

If Candlemas Day be fair and bright
Winter will have another fight.
If Candlemas Day brings cloud and rain,
Winter won't come again.
If Candlemas Day be dry and fair,
The half o the winter's to come and mair;
If Candlemas Day be wet and foul,
The half o the winter's gane at Yule.

Candlemas Bell Flowers
Gothic Gardening Blogger

Candlemas traditions and superstitions abound. Candlemas Bell flowers, also known as Snowdrops (galanthas nivalis), symbolize hope. The blooms of these delicate

flowers push their way up through the cold and snow blooming very early in the year, typically even before Candlemas. According to ancient folklore, it was believed that an angel helped these flowers to bloom and pointed them out to Eve as a sign of hope. Eve wept in repentance and sorrow at the cold and death that had come into the world as a result of what she had done. Many Christians also see these flowers as symbolizing the hope of Christ to the world. Some, however, believed Candlemas flowers brought in to the house prior to Candlemas Day would be unlucky and symbolized death or parting.

VALENTINE'S DAY - LEGENDS & LOVE

CANDLEMAS BRINGS LIGHT AND warmth to the home, and Valentine's Day brings warmth to the heart. Many myths surround this charming holiday with many claiming ties to the legendary St. Valentine, but one fact for certain is that recognition of the day dates to the time of the Roman Empire.

Valentine, a holy priest in Rome, was arrested for aiding Christian martyrs during the reign of Claudius II. The Emperor tried to get Valentine to renounce his Christian faith but failed and so ordered his execution but only after inflicting various means of punishment including beatings with clubs and being stoned. One of the crimes attributed to Valentine was continuing to marry young lovers during war time in defiance of the Emperor's law. The Emperor had recognized the reluctance of young lovers to go to

war, so he outlawed all marriages during war time.

Valentine's execution took place on February 14, 269 and in the ensuing years, he was canonized as a saint. In an event recorded years later, Valentine was credited with miraculously curing his jailer's blind daughter on the eve of his execution. This miracle attributed to him resulted in his canonization as a saint in the years following his death. Legend says Valentine signed a note to the young girl with, "From Your Valentine" – a phrase still used today. The legend of St. Valentine has grown through the centuries. From approximately 307 forward, the day has become a celebration of love and romance observed worldwide.

The fourteenth century found Valentine's Day being celebrated with a feast and Valentine greetings being sung. By the fifteenth century, Valentine messages were beginning to be written and given anonymously while the sixteenth century began the exchange of small tokens between lovers with the passing of a paper Valentine containing a handwritten note. The seventeenth century saw the day recognized with the sending of flowers, and by the mid-eighteenth century, Valentine's Day was celebrated with the exchanging of lavishly decorated handwritten notes.

How would Jane Austen and the young lovers in her novels have celebrated St. Valentine's Day? Intriguing thought indeed. Might Mr. Darcy have held with the traditional handwritten love note to Elizabeth? Would Captain Wentworth have slipped a small gift into Anne's hands anonymously or might Henry Tilney have delivered a cleverly written card to Catherine Moreland? One can

only surmise, but one of the most popular and beguiling methods of paying homage to one's sweetheart was with a puzzle purse.

A puzzle purse is made of origami-like paper carefully folded into a square determined by a preset pattern. The resulting folds of the square would often be numbered and read in order as each leaf was opened. A final message or picture would be found at the very center or "heart" of the puzzle. Such a wonderfully charming gift provided a rare and precious opportunity to convey a personal message or remembrance to one's sweetheart.

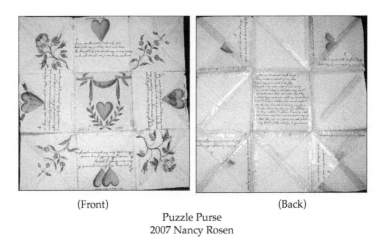

(Front)   (Back)

Puzzle Purse
2007 Nancy Rosen

Another favorite Valentine gift of the time bought by mariners and those who traveled, came to be known as "sailor's valentines." These beautiful pieces consist of one or, more often two, octagon-shaped wooden cases hinged together. Decorations made from varying types of small sea shells, seeds and other materials were glued to fabric inside the box to form a colorfully distinct design. Sailor's

valentines gained their name after thought to be the hand-iwork of sailors as a shipboard diversion from long days and even longer nights at sea. Fanciful traditions tell of these intricate pieces being made onboard ship as a home-coming gift for one's sweetheart.

The name "sailor's valentine" came into use mainly due to sentimental phrases included with the Valentine such as "With Love," "Be Mine," and "Forget Me Not." The octagonal shape is thought to come from old compass cases carried aboard sailing ships. Even though the thought of sailors crafting these heartfelt pieces sounds romantic, it's more likely that these pieces were created by John Fon-das who operated the New Curiousity Shop in Bridge-town, Barbados. The New Curiousity Shop was a popular souvenir shop where sailors were known to purchase gifts for their return home.Jane Austen had two sailor brothers, Francis and Charles, who traveled extensively on their voyages with the Royal Navy. Might they have purchased a "Sailor's Valentine" for their sweetheart, wife or even

Sailor's Valentine –"A Present/Think of Me", shell, cedar, glass, metal, cotton, tintype, ca. 1895. Courtesy of Strong Museum

possibly a gift for a dear sister? We know Jane and her brothers were close and that Charles gifted Jane and Cassandra with beautiful topaz crosses from his ship's prize earnings. He might have one day also gifted them with a lovely Sailor's Valentine. It warms one's heart to think of the possibility.

Cold February's holidays spread warmth, light and love. Whether celebrating Candlemas with the lighting of a candle or opening the folds of a puzzle purse from your sweetheart, both holidays bring warmth and peace to the sweet month of February. We linger here for a moment but our journey beckons us so off we go. Let's see how the raucous month of March might surprise and delight us.

March

Ladies, Legalities, & Mothers

When my Lord falls in my Lady's lap,
England, beware of some mishap!
English Proverb

LADY'S DAY

EVEN THOUGH LADY DAY seems a bit obscure and unfamiliar to us, it was actually of particular importance to members of the Regency Era. The observance of Lady Day began during the Middle Ages and carried an abundance of meanings. Lady Day, then and today, is observed on March 25th which is exactly nine months prior to the Christian observance of Christ's birth on December 25th. The "lady" of Lady Day was said to be the virgin Mary. It was believed that on this day the angel Gabriel appeared to Mary and announced that, even though a virgin, she was to be the mother of the Messiah.

Lady Day was originally known as Our Lady Day and became the first of four English quarter days. Lady Day was celebrated March 25th; Midsummer Day festivities held June 24th; Michaelmas Day recognized on September 29th; and Christmas Day observed December 25th. As few people could read and calendars were not yet common,

celebrations were typically held around the change of the seasons. Quarter days were placed at the same time as religious holidays which made them easier to remember.

Being the first of the four quarter days and coming at the beginning of spring, Lady Day was recognized during the Middle Ages as the start of a new year. This resulted in the day having great legal significance with all contracts for the upcoming year having to be signed by or on Lady Day. If you rented property, whether agricultural or lodgings in cities such as London or Bath, leases had to be signed by Lady's Day.

Cumbria England- Trek Earth

Work on tenant farms covered the span of one year to coincide with the harvest cycle so all necessary work could be finished. That meant the only time a tenant farmer would consider moving to a new farm would be after the harvest cycle was completed in the spring. Annual leases spanned the year from Lady Day to Lady Day so whether renewing a lease on an existing farm or signing a lease on a new farm, the contract would need to be completed and signed by Lady Day.

Lady Day also played a role during the London social season which typically began in late January or early February and ended in May. The "season" was critically important to young ladies hoping to secure an appropriate marriage with an eligible gentleman. Proper lodgings had to be secured by Lady Day to reflect the image of wealth and economic consequence vital to finding a wealthy husband. If obtaining suitable lodgings was not completed by March 25th, the success of the hopeful young lady's "season" might be in serious jeopardy.

For those of the superstitious bent, there was the dreaded possibility of Lady Day falling close to Easter which was possible in certain years since they both come at the first of spring. Should this coincidence happen, some thought it was a portent of bad fortune for England. Actually, this coincidence did happen in 1818 when Easter came on March 22nd, very early that year, and Lady Day followed in three short days. Queen Charlotte died in November later that year and her death was blamed on the two holidays coming so close together that year. These two holidays also came close together in 1853 and 1864 but happily, no devastating incidents occurred in England those two years.

A popular legend of Lady Day tells the tale of a lady of nobility and her traveling companions traversing the Great North Road one very dark night which ran through the village of St. Albans. Alas, they lost their way in the unfamiliar territory and darkness. In the distance, all they could see were lights on a far-away hilltop. They used the lights, which turned out to belong to a clock tower, to guide them to safety at the nearby monastery where they

found shelter for the night. The noble lady was so grateful for the kindness shown by the monks, she left money to be used to purchase cakes for the poor each year on Lady Day. Recorded in the 1900 edition of the *British Popular Customs – Present and Past* written by The Reverend T.F. Thiselton Dyer MA, these cakes are still distributed at St. Albans each Lady Day continuing the longstanding tradition established even before the time of the Regency Era.

Mothering Day

THREE WEEKS BEFORE EASTER, Regency Era dwellers would go "a-Mothering" in celebration of Mothering Day. Mothering Day was a day when visits were paid to each's "mother church" which was where one grew up attending or had been baptized. Children would often pick flowers to place in the church or to give to their mothers. It became a time when families were re-united as adults upon their return to their home village or town to attend a special church service. Many village young people went into service as household servants in large houses and Mothering Day was a holiday with time off from work. It was an important occasion for the family to be together since household servants were not typically given days off on other occasions.

Along with the church service, it was an opportunity to take a gift of clothing or food from your employer to your mother. The giving of such gifts and remembrances was the forerunner of today's tradition of giving gifts

to Mothers on Mother's Day. Girls might also bake their mother a "Simnel Cake" as a gift as commemorated in the poem by Robert Herrick in 1648.

'I'll to thee a Simnell bring
'Gainst thou go 'st a mothering,
So that, when she blesseth thee,
Half that blessing thou'lt give to me.'

Mothering Day fell on the fourth Sunday of Lent, the period from Ash Wednesday until Good Friday. Traditionally, a fast was observed during the time of Lent, however, the fast was lifted slightly on Mothering Sunday when a Simnel Cake was shared with family. A typical Simnel Cake was a light fruitcake with a layer of Marzipan baked into the middle and then, covered with another layer of marzipan on top. As part of the traditional Simnel Cake, decorations included 11 balls of marzipan representing the eleven apostles. Jesus Christ was included when 12 balls were used as decoration. According to legend, the Simnel Cake was named for Lambert Simnel who was said to have worked in the kitchens of Henry VII around 1500.

A different pastry related to Mothering Day around the turn of the century in 1600 was "Mothering Buns" also known as "Mothering Sunday Buns." These sweet buns were topped with pink or white icing and sprinkled with multi-colored sprinkles known in the United Kingdom as "hundreds and thousands."

What special holidays the month of March has shared with us! From Lady Day's religious and legal significance to Mothering Day bringing family members together, what a splendid time of year. We're off to April now as our travels continue. Let's see what sweet surprises await us. Step lively, Friend!

Simnel Cake

---※・※---

Prep: 30 MTS. Bake: 2 HRS. 30 MTS.

INGREDIENTS:

1 cup margarine softened

¼ cup candied mixed fruit peeled, chopped

1 cup light brown sugar

2 tablespoons grated lemon zest

4 eggs

2 teaspoons mixed spice

1 ¾ cup self-rising flour

1 pound almond paste

1 1/3 cup golden raisins

2 tablespoons apricot jam

1 cup dried currants

1 egg, beaten

2/3 cup candied cherries - rinsed, drained & quartered

DIRECTIONS:

Preheat oven to 300 degrees F (150 degrees C). Grease and flour an 8" spring form pan. Line the bottom and sides of pan with greased parchment paper.

In a large bowl, cream together the margarine and brown sugar until light and fluffy. Beat in the eggs one at a time. Beat in the flour. Stir in the golden raisins, currants, candied cherries, mixed fruit, lemon zest and mixed spice. Pour ½ of batter into prepared pan.

Divide almond paste into 3 equal portions. Roll out 1/3 of the almond paste to an 8" circle. Place the circle of almond paste on the cake batter in pan. Cover with remaining cake batter.

Bake in the preheated oven for 2 ½ hours, or until evenly brown and firm to the touch. If the cake is browning too quickly, cover with foil after an hour of baking. Let cool in pan for 10 minutes, then turn onto a wire rack and cool completely. Set oven to broil.

When the cake has cooled, brush the top with warmed apricot jam. Roll out 1/3 of the almond paste in an 8" circle and place on top of cake. Divide the remaining 1/3 of almond paste into 11 pieces and roll into balls. These represent the 11 apostles (excluding Judas). Brush the almond paste on top of cake with beaten egg. Arrange the 11 balls around the outside edge on top of cake. Brush the balls lightly with egg.

Place the cake under the broiler for 8-10 minutes, or until almond paste is golden brown.

AllRecipes.com

April

Dormant Winter Makes Way for Life-Giving Spring

"Mr. Weston . . . I believe he is one of the very best tempered men that ever existed . . . I shall never forget his flying Henry's kite for him that very windy day last Easter . . ."

Isabella Knightley ~ *Emma*

EASTER PRESENTS A UNIQUE predicament. It falls on a different date each year but comes sometime between March 22nd and April 25th. It is observed on the first Sunday after the first full moon following the first day of spring. This designation came about in 325 A.D by the "Easter Rule" determined by the Council of Nicaea called by Emperor Constantine. Since Easter can come in either March or April, let's start our little visit through April by taking a look at April Fool's Day first and then explore April's other intriguing holidays.

APRIL FOOL'S DAY

APRIL 1ST. IT SEEMS like such a silly little holiday but it has a rich and very old history. There are several theories as to the origin of the holiday but most historians tend toward the theory evolving around the

adaptation of the Gregorian calendar in 1752. Until then, April 1st was observed as the beginning of the new year coinciding with spring's arrival. But in 1752 when the Gregorian calendar was adopted, January 1st became the start of the new year. Those slow to learn of this change and could be led to believe April 1st was still the start of a new year, became the target of jokes and hoaxes. Some of the jokes played on these poor "fools" included paper fish being stuck to their back and called such names as "*poisson d'avril*" or "April fish." That meant you were a young, easily caught fish or someone who is gullible. April Fool's might also have been connected to the spring vernal equinox which was a time of year when Mother Nature could "fool" all by changing the weather and making it unpredictable.

Another fun possibility that history records dates back to Britain in 1698 when pranksters invited friends to the "washing of the white lions" at the Tower of London, the location where the Royal Menagerie was kept. The Royal Menagerie, begun in the early 1100s, consisted of exotic animals such as kangaroos, lions, elephants and ostriches kept as symbols of power and for the entertainment and curiosity of the royal court. In 1860, a young prankster thought it would be quite funny to repeat the earlier prank going to the extra effort of mailing invitations to the "washing of the white lions." Several curiosity seekers actually showed up but to their chagrin there were no lions there – let alone any that needed washing. The Menagerie had closed in 1835 when the remaining animals were moved to the Zoological Society of London's Regent Park.

Such pranks were only the beginning of a holiday that is

still celebrated worldwide with jokes and hoaxes and today, even some pranks that involve TV and radio broadcasts of outlandish fictional stories. Beware each April 1st to keep your wits about you lest you be the next poisson d'avril!

MAUNDY THURSDAY

THE SOLEMN, "CEREMONY OF the Royal Maundy" dating from the time of Edward I, takes place the Thursday evening before Easter Sunday and commemorates the last supper Christ had with His apostles. The term, "Maundy," is derived from the Latin *mandatum* meaning "command." It was a reference to Jesus' words in John where he tells His apostles: "And now a new commandment: love one another. As I have loved you, so you must love one another." Customary in England until 1689, the Monarch would wash the feet of the poor on the Thursday before Easter in Westminster Abbey. This act was symbolic of Christ's act of humility when He washed the feet of His apostles. It is interesting to note that the feet were washed first by Yeoman of the Laundry before they were washed – and kissed – by the Monarch. Food and clothing were also handed out to the poor that day.

In modern-day Britain, the Monarch still follows the traditional method first established by King Edward I in the 13th century of handing out Maundy money to senior pensioners. At one point, recipients had to be the same gender as the Monarch, but by the 18th century and the time of King Henry IV, recipients were the same number of

men as women. The number of recipients was determined by years of the Sovereign's age.

At the ceremony, Yeoman of the Guard carry Maundy money in red and white leather string purses on golden alms trays on their heads. Money in the red leather string purses is regular coinage – money in lieu of food and clothing. Coins in the white leather purses are specially-minted Maundy coins and total the same number of pence as years of the Monarch's age. Maundy money came into being at the time of King Charles in 1662 with undated, hammered coins; it wasn't until 1670 that the coins included dates. Maundy coins are legal tender struck in sterling silver and made especially for this annual ceremony which makes them highly sought after by collectors. Maundy money recipients are retired pensioners recommended by clergy and ministers of all denominations in recognition of good deeds and service to their church and community.

Queen Elizabeth on
Maundy Thursday
The British Standard

ST. GEORGE'S DAY

ST. GEORGE IS THE patron saint of England, an interesting fact considering he probably never even visited England. Legend tells the story that around 303 BCE, George, a high-ranking officer in the Roman army, was tortured and killed for his Christian faith. The torture

ordered by Roman Emperor Diocletian was cruel even by the standard of the time, but George courageously clung to his faith and was eventually beheaded near Lydda in Palestine.

Legends abound of St. George's courage and endurance and grew to include tales of his fighting and slaying a dragon. Of course, that battle probably never happened but the dragon was used since it often symbolized evil.

Twelfth century crusaders were thought to have been the first to invoke his name during battle. King Edward III named George as the Patron Saint of England in 1350 and formed the Order of the Garter in St. George's name. King Henry V advanced George's following further when he invoked his name at the battle of Agincourt in northern France in 1415. Some soldiers even declared they saw St. George among them as Agincourt was a spectacular victory for the British. Henry V was thought to embody many of the noble characteristics of St. George and was immortalized by Shakespeare in the play bearing his name with, "Cry God for Harry, England and St. George!"

In England, St. George, which means "earth worker or farmer" is celebrated in the spring on April 23rd at the time crops begin to grow. Through history, many in Europe have prayed to St. George for a good harvest. Today, on April 23rd, St. George's Day is celebrated with a feast and the flying of his flag.

Flag of St. George

EASTER

I N BRITAIN, THE CELEBRATION of Easter began long before Christianity arrived. Historians believe Easter was named for the Anglo-Saxon goddess, Eastre, goddess of the dawn and spring. The holiday's religious significance make it one of the most observed holidays on the calendar with traditional practices based on religious as well as original pagan practices.

Easter has always been a time of celebration marking an end to winter and Lent. Palm branches are waved in parades in the United Kingdom today just as they were waved to welcome royalty during the time of the Roman Empire and waved as Christ was welcomed into Jerusalem on His triumphal entry.

During the Regency Era, the Easter Season consisted of Easter and the 40 days following until Ascension Sunday which commemorated Christ's final ascension into heaven. This was a popular time for travel and visiting family. Every time the holiday was mentioned in Jane Austen's letters and novels, it involved family or characters in her novels traveling. In *Pride & Prejudice* in particular, Mr. Darcy and Colonel Fitzwilliam travel to Rosings to visit their Aunt Catherine Debourgh. As Jane Austen tells us, " . . . it was not till Easter-day, almost a week after the gentlemen's arrival, that they were honoured by such an attention and then they were merely asked on leaving church to come there in the evening."

The idea of wearing something new for Easter had its

roots in Roman tradition. It was said to bring good luck to wear something new in the spring and at the time, was considered a must for all those gently bred Regency ladies to wear a new gown of the latest fashion. Easter was also a traditional day for getting married so the wearing of something new as a bride and a new bonnet made with flowers and ribbons may have had its beginnings as Easter bonnets. The bonnets with their bright spring flowers would have been a welcome spot of color after the dreariness of winter and the somberness of Lent. The official London Season and its festive balls, parties and routs did not fully start until after Easter Sunday since such social events were not considered proper during Lent.

Easter celebrations during the Regency continued many of the ancient traditions dating back hundreds of years. One of the oldest traditions was the giving of decoratively-dyed, hard-boiled eggs as gifts with eggs having a long history associated  with fertility, birth and new life. Eggs were typically given up at Lent, so excess chicken eggs were hard boiled to make them last longer and to assure there being an abundance during Easter week. Legend tells the story of a nest of lark's eggs being gifted to St. Francis by the animals to show their love for him. A rabbit, said to be a constant companion of St. Francis and the earthly symbol for the goddess, Eastre, then asked the daffodil for its yellow color the crocus for its blue and the violet for its purple to

color the eggs. St. Francis was so pleased with the gift that he said a basket of colored eggs would return forever in memory of the first Eastre rabbit.

Regency Era inhabitants used natural resources as dyes for hardboiled eggs. Decorative patterns were created using a blade to carefully scratch dye off to create a pattern by allowing the white of the egg shell to show through. Others placed tallow or wax on the egg shell to create a pattern. The tallow was then peeled off after the dying to reveal the design. "Egg Rolling" was a favorite Easter game where children and adults alike rolled their dyed, hard-boiled eggs down a hill with the winner being the egg that rolled the farthest.

Spring time always brings an abundance of lovely blooming flowers and one of great significance to Easter celebrations is the daffodil also known as the Lent Lily. The daffodil is the symbol of rebirth and new beginnings and its  distinctive yellow trumpet is a colorful sign of spring. The Lent Lily is said to bloom on Ash Wednesday and die on Easter Day as immortalized in A.E. Housman's famous poem, *The Lent Lilly:*

The Lent Lily

'Tis spring; come out to ramble
The hilly brakes around,
For under thorn and bramble
About the hollow ground
The primroses are found.

And there's the windflower chilly
With all the winds at play,
And there's the Lenten lily
That has not long to stay
And dies on Easter day.

And since till girls go maying
You find the primrose still,
And find the windflower playing
With every wind at will,
But not the daffodil,

Bring baskets now, and sally
Upon the spring's array,
And bear from hill and valley
The daffodil away
That dies on Easter day.

~ A.E. Housman

And what food would inhabitants of the Regency Era enjoy while celebrating Easter? The Easter dinner would have included ham or lamb and of course, hot cross buns, reputedly the most famous Easter delicacy. Hot Cross Buns

are small, lightly sweet yeast buns that include raisins, currants and possibly other kinds of chopped fruit. Before baking, a slash would be cut across the top of the bun to symbolize the cross on which Christ died. After baking, the slash on top would be filled with confectioner sugar icing. Hot Cross Buns were a special treat and children would sing an old rhyme while anticipating the favorite:

"Hot cross buns,
Hot cross buns,
one a penny, two a penny,
hot cross buns.

If you do not like them,
give them to your son,
one a penny, two a penny
hot cross buns."

Hot Cross Bun Seller
Jane Austen Center

The first mention of Hot Cross Buns comes in Poor Robin's Almanack in 1733: "Good Friday comes this month the old woman runs, with one or two a penny hot cross buns." The buns are baked and eaten on Good Friday leading up to Easter Sunday. English tradition says that a bun baked on Good Friday would bring good luck all year to the household and would not mold. Some buns were even kept through the year until

the next batch was made.

What an array of holidays April has shared with us and each one such a treat! Our holiday journey is so enlightening – so many wonderful holidays to explore. Let's hurry on to discover what the month of May has in store for us.

Hot Cross Buns at Fortnum & Mason, Piccadilly, April 2010,
courtesy of Wikimedia Commons.

Hot Cross Buns

INGREDIENTS:

1 cup milk

¼ teaspoon cinnamon

4 teaspoons water

¼ teaspoon nutmeg, grated

1 cake fresh yeast

1 egg beaten

3 cups all-purpose flour

¼ cup melted butter

1/3 cup sugar

1 cup currants

1 teaspoon salt

DIRECTIONS:

Heat milk and water to lukewarm.

Crumble yeast, mix with ½ cup flour. Stir in tepid milk/water and mix well.

Cover and set aside in a warm place until the yeast is active and frothing – about 10-15 minutes.

Mix remaining flour sugar salt, cinnamon and nutmeg.

Stir egg and butter into yeast mix, add the flour mixture and fruit. Mix well.

Put dough onto a floured surface and knead well; return to bowl and let rise until double in bulk, about an hour.

Turn onto a floured surface and knead again.

Preheat oven to 375 degrees.

Divide dough into 12 pieces and shape into buns; mark a deep cross on the top of each bun.

Arrange on a baking tray, cover with a tea towel, and let rise for 30 minutes. Cook in preheated 375 degree oven for 15 minutes or until golden brown.

Jane Austen Centre Newsletter
Issue 10 – Laura Boyle

Happy Birthday!

"I wish you joy of your birthday twenty times over."
Jane Austen in a letter to her sister, Cassandra ~ January 8, 1799

BIRTHDAYS. WE ALL HAVE them once a year. We usually celebrate with cake and candles, presents, birthday cards and occasionally a grand party. This type of celebration hasn't always been the case though. The Regency Era was so diverting with extravagant excesses in so many things, but excesses in birthdays (well, most birthdays) . . . not so much.

So . . . just how did they celebrate birthdays (if they did), during the Regency Era? A lot depended on your social status. The higher up the social ladder you were, the more elaborate your birthday celebration but . . . let's start at the other end of the spectrum with the very poor. The poor, working class may have celebrated their children's

birthdays with a gift of a piece of candy or other small token. On the next rung up the ladder, the children may have been allowed to sit at the parents' table that night for dinner rather than eating in the nursery. If you were an heir or the firstborn of the gentry class, there may have been a large party or ball given in your honor and the first birthday would have been celebrated the grandest of all. As for royalty, their birthdays were celebrated as national holidays and were also the cause for significant social events such as signaling the start of the London social season. For example, Queen Charlotte's birthday was celebrated in January or February to mark the beginning of the "season" but her actual birthday wasn't until May.

The Prince Regent was in a category of extravagance all his own when he held a fete (supposedly in honor of his father, King George's, birthday) in 1811. The Prince Regent's wildly extravagant party at Carlton House, the royal residence, was lauded by those fortunate to be invited and condemned as unneeded extravagance by those in opposition. Over 2,000 people were invited, and the observer was said to have been struck with astonishment at the exorbitance on display. The dance floor for this royal gala was "chalked," a custom popular among the most wealthy from 1808 to 1821. An intricate pattern drawn in chalk on this particular dance floor, included King George's initials in the center. The extravagance of the chalked patterns was evident once the dancing began as shoes and slippers scuffed the pattern until it was no longer distinguishable. Flowing descriptions of the dinner, the Prince's field marshal's uniform, the elaborate decorations and the sheer

number of attendees merited a place in the record book of birthday celebration excesses.

In contrast, mentions of birthdays in Jane Austen's letters were low key and never included an indication of how they might have been celebrated. We do know, however, Jane Austen received a very significant gift on her nineteenth birthday. According to biographer, David Nokes, "For her nineteenth birthday, Mr. Austen bought Jane 'a small mahogany writing desk with 1 long drawer and glass ink stand compleat' which he purchased from Ring's of Bastingstoke for 12 (shillings)." What gift could have been more momentous to the future literary master.

So, from the excesses of a royal Prince Regent exhibiting his wealth and power to a heartfelt gift from a father to a daughter, the disparity in birthday celebrations was wide. No matter the way in which an individual's birthday was celebrated, the special occasion was acknowledged in some way, whether it was small or grand, it was almost certainly heartfelt.

It's time to leave the birthday party and continue on as we step into the flower-scented month of May.

which was thought to help the sun strengthen its spring-time warmth. The promising allure of a new fire caused sweethearts to walk through its smoke believing it would bring good luck. Cattle were driven through the smoke to invoke its cleansing effect while travelers were known to jump over fires in the hope of safe journeys. Even babies were carried across dying embers to keep them well. With the strong powers the setting of a new fire conjured, it was conversely thought to be especially bad luck to ask anyone for a start of fire from their hearth on the first of May. You might even be thought a witch if you asked!

The first of May was also important to the Romans who occupied the British Isles beginning around 43 AD. They brought with them the observance of the Feast of Floralia, the goddess of flowers. Through the years, the customs of the Festivals of Beltrane and Floralia became intertwined and gradually evolved into the more well-known obser-vances of May Day.

As a lingering custom from the celebration of the Feast of Floralia, people would rise long before sunrise and gath-er fresh flowers and blooms. The fresh flowers decorated homes and were strewn across doorsteps in the hope of bringing good fortune to the home's inhabitants. Marsh mallow and primrose petals were especially potent pro-tection. It was also believed that hanging mountain ash around doorways would safeguard the home from harm. While it was popular to use flowers in the hopes of invok-ing security, it was also popular to gather branches of bud-ding blooms and flower bouquets to give as gifts.

In France, King Charles IX of France was given a lily-

of-the-valley on May 1st, 1561 as a good luck charm. At the King's initiation, the custom soon began to give a sprig of lily-of-the-valley to ladies of the royal court each year on May 1st. By the start of the 20th century, it was customary to give a sprig of lily-of-the-valley to loved ones on May 1st to mark the start of spring, a tradition which continues today.

Come Join in the May Pole Dance
Henry John Yeend King

One of the most recognizable traditions surrounding May Day is the dancing around the Maypole by dancers carrying long streams of ribbons. The dance resulted in the weaving of a beautiful and intricate pattern around the pole. The Maypole celebration began long before daybreak on May 1st with the cutting of the Maypole tree. For centuries, trees have been the symbol of nature's strength and fertility and their use in ancient rituals have made them the centerpiece of many festivals. Branches were lopped off and long streamers of ribbons tied to the top. The pole was then brought in to the village at sunrise with dancing

to the music of horns and flutes. The pole could be of any size but villages were known to compete for the tallest and grandest possible. In smaller villages and communities, Maypole trees were cut from the forest annually for the May 1st festivities, but in larger cities, permanent Maypoles were left standing year round.

The May Queen was the symbolic human replica of the Goddess Flora, and her crowning was the highlight of the day. Following established tradition, the Queen would regally watch her "subjects" dance and play games from the comfort of a flower-covered throne.

Following nature's lead with its fresh flowers and lush green growth, loveliness and youth were prominent on this day. An old folk tale says fair maidens would be made even more fair by rising early in the morning and washing their faces in the dew which was believed to make them beautiful throughout the year. An ancient English proverb says, "The fair maid who the first of May, goes to the fields at the break of day, and washes in dew from the hawthorn tree, will ever handsome be."

The stringing of May garlands was also popular among young girls while groups of young men might lift fair maidens high in flower bedecked chairs. The maiden would then have opportunity to make her pick from the young men the next day.

In northern England, May 1st was the day, if you should choose, to pull some late "April fooling" pranks. If you "tricked" someone in May, you called out "May Gosling!" The typical response would be, "May Goslings past and gone. You're the fool for making me one!"

May Day may not be as heartily celebrated in North America as it is in Europe but dancing around the Maypole, crowning a May Queen and hanging baskets of flowers on door knobs have survived as part of ancient English rituals observed through the centuries.

Jane Austen took notice of and enjoyed the beautiful, fresh flowers of spring too. She wrote of spring flowers in bloom at Chawton House in a letter to her sister, Cassandra, in May 1811, "Our young Piony at the foot of the Fir tree has just blown and looks very handsome; & the whole of the Shrubbery Border will soon be gay with Pinks & Sweet Williams, in addition to the Columbines already in bloom. The Syringas too are coming out." Let's join Jane as we pause for a moment and take a deep breath. Enjoy the soft scent of fresh flowers floating on a gentle evening's breeze, soft and gentle, and the flowers so sweet. It's hard to leave this beautiful place, but there are many holidays waiting to be explored so with a fond farewell, we bid adieu as May with its lovely, petaled flowers and ribbon-strewn poles gently eases us into the shimmering warmth of summer and the month of June.

June

Fire, Fairies and the Summer Solstice

"Whatever is dreamed this night will come to pass."
"Midsummer Night's Dream"
William Shakespeare

T HE SUMMER SOLSTICE, ALSO known as Midsummer, is highly mysterious and deeply magical. As with some other festivals, it was believed to be a time when spirits wandered more freely and powerful spiritual forces were at work. Activities of spirits and fairies were supposed to be at their high point, passing between worlds as the hours between twilight

Midsummer's Eve
John William Waterhouse

and dawn on this day were thought to be closest to the underworld. Such was the basis of Shakespeare's immortal play, *Midsummer Night's Dream,* often performed in theaters across England on Midsummer's Eve and Midsummer's Night. It was a holiday celebrated much as we celebrate

New Year's Eve today and folk lore abounds surrounding its rituals and festivals.

Solstice is a Latin term derived from the words *sol* (sun) and *sistere* (to stand still). The summer solstice is the midpoint of the year and marks the year's longest day when the sun seems to hang in the sky for hours. The summer solstice, established by tradition, is the year's high water mark making it the middle day of the year and the noon hour as the middle hour of the year. In *Emma*, Jane Austen makes prominent use of Midsummer holiday timing when the characters visit Donwell Abbey in the summer to pick strawberries. Naming the Midsummer holiday itself, she also mentions the noon hour, the middle hour of the year, when she says, "Under a bright mid-day sun, at almost Midsummer, Mr. Woodhouse was safely conveyed in his carriage, with one window down, to partake of this *al-fresco* party . . ."

With the height of the year being at Midsummer, all days following would grow shorter until, in contrast, the winter solstice, known as Yule, would be celebrated as the shortest day of the year. The winter and summer solstices have been used through the centuries to mark the easternmost sunrise and the westernmost sunset. Hundreds of ancient stone circles are testament to the various rituals that pay homage to the sun's path across the sky. One of the most famous stone circles, Stonehenge, is said to be aligned on the midwinter *setting* sun and the midsummer *rising* sun.

Beginning with the ancient Celts, the June 24th summer solstice was celebrated with the lighting of fires and

bonfires across the countryside. Fires were used to entice the sun to stay in the sky longer. Lit with the charred remains of the previous year's logs, animal bones would often be burned for good fortune. The word "bonfire" is the combination of two words: "bone" and "fire" and a blazing fire was thought to bring good luck.

With the coming of Christianity, the summer solstice festival was adapted into another important celebration, the birth of John the Baptist, and became known as St. John's Day. Tradition held that the bright yellow flowers of St. John's Wort, symbolized the luster of the sun, and the spots of red on the flowers symbolized the blood of the martyred John the Baptist. Its association with John the Baptist and St. John's Day brought this sweet little flower to prominence. Wreaths of St. John's Wort were hung on the horns of cattle and sheds decorated with the flower for protection.

Wreaths were allowed to "die with the sun" and spores from dead ferns were thought to be bring about miraculous knowledge and power. It was believed that all herbs were especially potent at Midsummer so it was a popular time for making medicines and potions. Young ladies would place a sprig or two of flowers under their pillows in hopes that magical dreams of future loves would come to them in the night.

Whether Regency Era dwellers participated in Midsummer observances or festivities, its place on the calendar was used as a defining marker for day-to-day life. In *Sense and Sensibility*, Mrs. Jennings, ever playing the matchmaker, thought she detected an attachment between

Colonel Brandon and Elinor Dashwood and when the match did not happen as quickly as she thought, "instead of Midsummer, they would not be married till Michaelmas, and by the end of a week, that it would not be a match at all." (*Sense & Sensibility*, Chp. 32) Or in *Emma*, talking of Jane Fairfax's changing plans for the summer: "Jane had come to Highbury professedly for three months; the Campbells were gone to Ireland for three months, but now the Campbells had promised their daughter to stay at least till Midsummer, and fresh invitations had been issued to join them there." (*Emma*, Chp. 33)

We've experienced the magic and the mysteriousness of June and its Midsummer revelries. This beguiling month holds even more delights in store as we move on to learn of June's charm as the traditional month for weddings.

Happily Wedded Bliss

"You must and shall be married by a special license!"
Mrs. Bennett about Elizabeth's wedding to Mr. Darcy
Pride & Prejudice

WHETHER DURING REGENCY TIMES or today, what lovelier event is there than a wedding? The bride is radiant. The groom nervously beams his excitement. The families are all smiles and the guests all twitter with anticipation as the happy couple "tie the knot."

Regency Era brides, just like brides of today, had many of the same decisions to make for their wedding and its celebration. What was the bride going to wear? What was served at the wedding breakfast or today, the reception, lunch or dinner? Were there bridesmaids and groomsmen? So many similarities and yet so many variances! And just as Mrs. Bennett thought upon leaving the Netherfield Ball, "Mrs. Bennet was perfectly satisfied, and quitted the house under the delightful persuasion that, allowing for the necessary preparations of settlements, new carriages, and wedding-clothes, she should undoubtedly see her daughter settled at Netherfield in the course of three or four months." (*Pride & Prejudice*, Chp. 18)

After months of courtship with only bits of private conversation between the couple, the Regency engagement itself was a sedate affair. There was no proposal on bended knee or engagement ring. The engagement came about as a result of conversation where the couple came to a mutually-happy agreement. Engagements weren't considered official until the father of the prospective bride was approached by the groom where he asked for the young lady's hand in marriage. The father then granted (or sometimes not) his permission. It was typically with great trepidation the groom approached his potential father-in-law. Even with his wealth and social standing, Mr. Darcy in *Pride & Prejudice,* sought the consent of Mr. Bennett. "During their walk, it was resolved that Mr. Bennett's consent should be asked in the course of the evening . . . soon after Mr. Bennett withdrew to the library, she (Elizabeth) saw Mr. Darcy rise also and follow him, and her agitation on seeing it was extreme . . . Mr. Darcy appeared again, when, looking at him, she was a little relieved by his smile." (Chp. 59) Some young men today still follow this time-honored course of action and there are some who still proceed without officially gaining approval of the bride's parents.

Did an engagement ring mark a Regency Era engagement? That answer to us would be a surprising "no." A diamond ring was not part of the traditional engagement process in Regency England. It was considered proper though for a bride to give her fiancé a small portrait of herself for him to carry. If the engagement should be one of long duration, such as an engagement between younger people, it was permissible for the bride to give the groom

a ring with a lock of her hair as a remembrance until they married. Jane Austen made note of this tradition by the ring Lucy Steele gave Edward Ferrars in *Sense and Sensibility*. Lucy tells Elinor Dashwood, with some devious intent, "Yes, I have one other comfort in his picture, but poor Edward has not even that. If he had but my picture, he says he would be easy. I gave him a lock of my hair set in a ring when he was in Longstaple last . . ." (Chp. 22) The groom, interestingly though, did not give a gift to his bride during the engagement period.

The couple agreed to marry and the father gives his consent, and now that the engagement is official, the seriousness of the commitment begins in earnest. This period became a time when the young couple could sit together and engage in more private, but still chaperoned, time together and small gifts or tokens of affection could be exchanged. While an opportunity to get to know each other better, the courtship period was also the time for legalities surrounding the union to take place and official announcements made in the parish to make way for the coming nuptials.

The legalities included all facets of monetary affairs for the new couple. Negotiations for "settlement papers" were typically handled by lawyers with requests and desires supplied by the groom and father of the bride. When a young lady married, everything, and that means *everything*, became property of the groom. Negotiations were conducted on every item feasible including the bride's dowry, pin money, children and what happened in the event of the husband's death. A dowry was the amount

of money the bride's father would entrust to his daughter's future husband on her behalf. For those of wealthier families, the dowry was an impressive amount which undoubtedly enhanced the young lady's appeal to suitors. In less affluent families, the father would be hard pressed to provide a dowry sufficient enough to impress possible courters. Every effort would be given to make it as substantial a sum as possible which could very well determine the future status of his daughter.

After the dowry amount was determined, the next item of negotiation was pin money. Pin money was an important factor and was to be provided to the wife on a regular basis throughout her married life. The use of the pin money was solely up to the wife, and she could use the money for such things as clothes, jewelry or gifts. Mrs. Bennett in *Pride & Prejudice* is quite beside herself at the thought of Lizzie's pin money upon her marriage to Mr. Darcy. "Oh, my sweetest Lizzy! how rich and how great you will be! What pin-money, what jewels, what carriages you will have!" (Chp. 59) The wealthier the husband, of course, the more pin money available to the bride.

It might seem an odd thing for negotiations to be held concerning future children, but it included provisions for the dowries of future daughters and the inheritance amounts for future sons. Plans would already be in place for children, removing potential future worry on how they would be provided for should unseen circumstances happen.

As for death provisions, it was not a topic young lovers would want to dwell upon but a necessity nonetheless. Provisions, called the "jointure," were made for the

wife should her future husband precede her in death. Such things were detailed such as where the wife could expect to live, provisions for minor children, the wife's allowance and distribution of valuables such as art, jewelry, clothing, etc. In reading novels and letters from the Regency Era, one can't help but see repeatedly how important these provisions and negotiations were to both successful courtship and to a young lady's future security and if necessary, independence.

Once legalities were satisfactorily negotiated, formalization of the vows was the next step. If the couple was to marry in the Church of England, typically the case during the Regency Era, the publishing of the banns was the next step in announcing the upcoming marriage. This was an announcement of the upcoming marriage made during church services for three consecutive Sundays in the local parish church. If the bride and groom were from different parishes, the banns were to be read in both parishes on the same three Sundays. Following the three readings, wedding vows could be performed at any time during the next 90 days, however, vows could not be solemnized until certification was received from the other parish, if necessary, stating banns had been "thrice called" and no objections received. Announcing banns at the local parish could pose a risk though as public objections could be made by anyone venturing to do so.

The Bann would read:

PUBLISH the Banns of Marriage between M. of _____ and N. of _____. If any of you know cause, or just impediment, why these two persons should not be joined together in holy Matrimony, ye are to declare it. This is the first [second, or third] time of asking.

If the couple wished to avoid the reading of the public banns or handle the engagement more privately, they could simply purchase a Common/Ordinary license from a bishop or archbishop at a cost of around 10 shillings.

The third method, a special license, was the most expensive way to solemnize vows and was typically used by the more well-to-do. It cost four to five pounds and ultimately issued at the discretion of the archbishop. It gave the couple considerable freedom, allowing them to marry in any parish and at any time of their choosing.

The fourth and what most considered most ignoble way to marry, was to elope. Couples who didn't want to wait for banns to be read, couldn't afford either type of license or had other mitigating circumstances were known to head to Gretna Green, a small town just across the border into Scotland. Marriage rules in the Scottish Presbyterian Church were not as strict as those in the Church of England so couples could marry in Gretna Green by simply pledging themselves to their partner in the presence of another person. On this pretext, anyone could conduct the wedding ceremony and this person was oftentimes Gretna Green's blacksmith. The slang term for marrying in Gretna Green become known as "marrying over the anvil" and blacksmiths became known as "anvil

priests." Eloping was a source of social embarrassment and shame to the families just as the elopement of Wickham and Lydia caused such great distress in the Bennett family in *Pride & Prejudice*.

While the reading of the banns was going on at church and legal negotiations were taking place at the lawyer's office, the bride and her mother were busy making selections for the bride's trousseau. The same big question then as today: What is the bride going to wear? Mrs. Bennett was certainly concerned what Lydia should wear for her potential wedding when she exclaimed, "And as for wedding-clothes, do not let them wait for that, but tell Lydia she shall have as much money as she chuses to buy them, after they are married." (*Pride & Prejudice*, Chp. 47) Of course, much of the bride's ensemble would depend on her financial circumstances. Dresses were precious commodities so those from the lower to middle classes, would usually pick one of their nicest dresses to wear. The dress would typically be worn again after the wedding, so the bride might add a touch of something new such as lace or trim to make it distinctive for her wedding day. Bonnets, much like those routinely worn when outdoors or attending church were also popular for the bride to wear. Wedding veils during the Regency period were optional but if worn, were usually attached to a coronet of flowers or a short veil was attached to a bonnet. A full veil worn over the face was thought to shield the bride from evil spirits and prevent the bad luck of the groom seeing the bride before vows were exchanged. Happily, by the Regency Era, this custom had waned and veils were common as a stylish part of head dresses for formal occasions.

For brides of the well-to-do and aristocracy, one's wedding dress and accessories were typically bought or made specifically for the wedding but also made with the current fashion and style in mind so the dress could be worn on special occasions later. Wedding dresses of the wealthy may have tended to be more elaborate, made of costly fabric and could also have been embellished with lace work and embroidery. Too much embellishment would have been frowned upon by society at the time. It was thought that what was worn should reflect the soberness of the wedding occasion. What a contrast to what

Shoe, c. 1795-1800, in the Museum of the City of New York; gift of Clarence F. Michalis.

must have been at Mrs. Elton's wedding in *Emma* as she comments on the Emma's and Mr. Knightley's wedding, "Mrs. Elton, from the particulars detailed by her husband, thought it all extremely shabby, and very inferior to her own. "Very little white satin, very few lace veils..." (Chp. 55) So then, it is left to the imagination how much white satin and how many lace veils there must have been at Mrs. Elton's wedding.

And what about the color? Most aristocratic wedding brides wore gowns of silver, gold or of expensive fabrics in deep, rich colors. Accessories would have matched the elaborateness of the bride's gown and might have included tall gloves, slippers to match the wedding dress, silk stockings, jewelry and a head covering such as a bonnet with flowers or a veil. As wedding dresses were typically worn

as regular clothing after the wedding, it was necessary for the bride to have something else as a keepsake of the day. This keepsake would probably have been one of her wedding shoes since shoes were considered good luck. Notes attached to the instep of satin slippers were carefully inscribed with remembrances of the wearer's wedding day.

A bouquet of flowers completed the bride's ensemble. Significant by introducing an element of nature into the wedding, flowers also conveyed implications of long-held beliefs in pagan fertility. Unless brides lived in larger cities with flowers available in shops or from street vendors, the bride's bouquet would often be fresh flowers picked from her family's own garden or garden of a neighbor.

As for the groom's attire, his ensemble was not as involved as the bride but a wedding called for something dressier than typical daily wear. As weddings took place during the morning hours, donning formal evening attire for the occasion was fitting for the groom. A groom might wear a white shirt with a snow-white cravat tied at the neck in an elaborate knot and a simple but tasteful tie pin. The shirt would be accompanied by a pair of dark or buff-colored breeches buckled right below the knee. Long trousers were gradually coming into fashionable evening wear during this period so either breeches or trousers might be worn by the groom. If the groom wore breeches buckled below the knee, he would also probably

wear natural-colored silk stockings with a pair of black pump shoes. Boots were not thought to be formal enough to wear to a wedding. To top it all off, a close-fitting, well-cut jacket would be donned possibly made of embroidered silk-satin or uncut velvet worn in a cut away or swallow-tail style and left open to display the selected waistcoat. If the groom desired, jackets, breeches or waistcoats could be worn in silver, white or blue.

The wedding itself would take place between the prescribed canonical hours of 8:00 a.m. and 12:00 noon and would take place in the home of the bride or parish church. If the wedding was to be held in the village parish, the couple would either walk or ride in a carriage to the ceremony, and would probably have arrived at the church separately to follow the tradition of the groom not seeing the bride before the wedding to insure good luck. The bride might have a couple of attendants who were young unmarried sisters or cousins and the groom a close friend or two as attendants. Attendees at even the most fashionable weddings would be only close family or friends or close friends from the village might be among the guests if the wedding was held at the village church.

Once at the church, the solemnity of the occasion set a tone of hushed silence. The father of the bride would most probably have escorted his daughter down the aisle, "giving her away," continuing a long-standing custom. Some also claim the bride walked the aisle alone while others say the groom escorted her. However, during the Regency Era, just like today, the bride and groom could change certain parts of the service to fit their preferences so there is no definitive

method of how the bride made it down the aisle. Suffice it to say, made it she did and once the bride and groom were at the alter, the solemn ceremony began.

The vows exchanged by characters in Jane Austen's novels were typically those traditionally exchanged by all couples in the Church of England. The ceremony came from "The Solemnization of Matrimony" section of *The Book of Common Prayer*, originally published in 1549. The wedding ring was an integral part of the wedding ceremony in the Church of England and in fact, a wedding couldn't be performed without one. The ring placed on the bride's finger during the ceremony was usually the first gift given by the groom to the bride and was typically a plain gold band but it could potentially be of any design and any metal.

Once the ceremony was completed, communion taken and appropriate responses made by the bride and groom, the couple would sign the parish registry in front of witnesses. The signing concluded on the same solemn note on

Signing the Registry
Edmund Blair Leighton

which the ceremony began but when the church doors opened . . . the celebration began. The couple, followed by a crowd of family and friends shouting well wishes, would make their way back to a predetermined location to celebrate with the traditional wedding "breakfast."

Since the ceremony was typically held early in the day, the wedding meal was the time for wedding attendees to "break their fast" or have breakfast. The menu varied widely for what was served at the breakfast and usually came down to the bride's desires, regional tastes and probably what the bride's family could afford.

No matter what else might be on the menu, one thing sure to be served was wedding cake. Regency Era wedding cakes were typically single-layered plum or fruit cakes containing large amounts of spices and alcohol which were prevalent to serve as preservatives. It was important to share a piece of wedding cake with as many friends and family as possible so preservatives were needed to help the cake survive being sent to absent guests. Tradition also tells us young ladies would sleep with a piece of wedding cake under their pillows, carefully wrapped in napkins, hoping to dream of the man they would marry someday. Jane Austen asks Cassandra in a letter October 1808, "Do you recollect whether the Manydown family send about their wedding cake? Mrs. Dundas has set her heart upon having a piece from her friend, Catherine."

Entertainment was part of the wedding festivities whether an individual musician or a larger musical group. Depending on the social status of the couple and their families, large dances or soirees might be held in their honor and poorer village families might celebrate with a bit of community revelry. It was customary to wish the new couple good luck as they departed the festivities by throwing shoes at their carriage. It was thought to be especially lucky if a shoe actually hit the carriage!

As for the carriage, it was considered proper etiquette for the groom to purchase a new carriage to convey his bride from the church door and then use on the ensuing bridal tour following the honeymoon. In *Sense and Sensibility,* Mr. Willoughby had a new carriage made for his wedding according to Mrs. Palmer. "The rest of Mrs. Palmer's

Wedding Breakfast
Regency Life

sympathy was shewn in procuring all the particulars in her power of the approaching marriage, and communicating them to Elinor. She could soon tell at what coachmaker's the new carriage was building, by what painter Mr. Willoughby's portrait was drawn, and at what warehouse Miss Grey's clothes might be seen." (Chp. 32) On the other hand, there is Mr. Rushworth in *Mansfield Park,* about which Jane Austen writes with her typical wit, "It was a very proper wedding ... nothing could be objected to when it came under discussion of the neighborhood except the carriage which conveyed the bride and groom from the church door ... it was the same chaise which Mr. Rushworth had used a twelvemonth before. In everything else, the etiquette of the day might stand the strictest investigation." (Chp. 21) It doesn't sound like a very good beginning for Mr. Rushworth.

The "honeymoon" was the couple's first month of

marriage, or one cycle of the moon. They might spend this time in their new home and in the following month or two embark on the customary bridal tour. The newlyweds would pay visits to members on both sides of the family, introducing the new family member to those who were unable to attend the wedding.

And of course, the most important item for the social scene, the wedding announcement, must be placed in the papers. As Jane Austen states to Anna LeFroy in a late February or early March letter in 1815, "Miss Blackford is married but I have never seen it in the Papers. And one may as well be single if the Wedding is not to be in print."

Once the wedding tour was completed, the couple settled into their home to start their new life together. We send our congratulations and best wishes after enjoying a delightful time preparing for and enjoying a lovely wedding. But now we journey on as we find out what beguiling holidays July holds in store.

Summertime Travel, Strawberries and Picnics

"I had the agreeable surprise of finding several scarlet strawberries quite ripe —had you been at home, this would have been a pleasure lost!
Jane Austen in a letter to her sister, Cassandra ~ 1811

REGENCY ERA DWELLERS SHOOK off the stifling city heat during the summer months and travelled to country houses and estates to enjoy the pastoral beauty and fresh air of life in the country. These journeys often provided opportunities for visiting friends and relations or were holiday tours to vacation destinations throughout England. Popular vacation locales included the seaside resort town of Brighton and the lure of the curative healing powers of the waters of Bath.

The sleepy little fishing village originally known as Brighthelmstone evolved into one of the most fashionable resorts in England with the modernized name of Brighton. Brighton first came to prominence as a seaside resort in the 1740s and 50s when Dr. Richard Russell of Lewes started prescribing the seawater of Brighton as a remedy for his patients' ills. Brighton gained even more distinction in the 1780s when the young Prince Regent made his own visit to Brighton for health reasons and took quite a liking to the

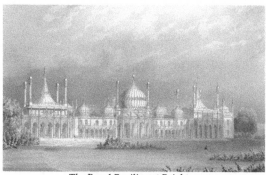

The Royal Pavilion at Brighton
John Nash

fashionable locale. He built an extravagant royal palace, the Royal Pavilion, at a turbulent time in England's history after the country had just come through the American Revolutionary War and the Napoleanic War with the French. The Prince Regent's extravagance at such a time raised the ire of some of his subjects. The flamboyant Prince, however, was not concerned. With his arrival and residence in Brighton, the city's social scene boomed with the opening of the Theatre Royal, the Brighton Dome and St. Anne's Well Spa. It was only natural that London's social elite, and social hopefuls, would follow so Brighton continued to transform into one of the most popular summer travel destinations during the Regency Era.

From the time the Romans dedicated Bath's springs to the Celtic god, Sul in 50 BC, the mineral springs have lured the sick to their waters. Bath had other major industries through the years including a successful wool industry, but it's steady and ever-popular attraction was its mineral springs. Queen Anne visited Bath in the early 1700s to "take the waters" and with those royal visits, Bath's official

ascent into resort town status began.

Jane Austen lived in Bath for a short time and two of her novels famously use locations in and around Bath. Bath's most distinguishing feature, what Regency Era visitors would have seen and visitors still see today, is the Royal Crescent. Its

Bath – Royal Crescent
Glyn Martin

semi-elliptical curve and Palladian architecture, have been and continue to be a wonder and delight. The grand Crescent became the centerpiece of Bath and was soon joined by the Pump Rooms, Assembly Rooms, Guild Hall and Theatre Royal. Jane was not very fond of busy, noisy Bath and her writing suffered and unfortunately, slowed while she lived there.

Brighton and Bath were not the only two resorts popular in England during the Regency Era but they were definitely two of the most popular. Summer visits, though, weren't confined to large resort cities. There could also be trips to the lovely countryside much like the trip to the north Elizabeth and the Gardiners took in *Pride & Prejudice*. Forays into the English countryside provided the opportunity for city dwellers to enjoy beautiful scenery and resplendent natural beauty. Majestic summer houses owned by the gentry were popular destinations for the socially astute and the swirl of entertainment and activities

for the visitors rivaled the social scene in London. As lovely and inviting as the country houses were, it was oftentimes the outdoors that appealed most. As Mrs. Gardiner says of Pemberley in trying to persuade Elizabeth to visit, "If it were merely a fine house richly furnished, . . . I should not care about it myself, but the grounds are delightful." (*Pride & Prejudice*, Chp. 42) And naturally, the grounds were just as appealing and grand as the house itself.

For those lucky enough to enjoy a summer outing or a visit to a country home, walking through the garden gate offered sights, sounds and delicious floral scents not available in the city. Even though the summer temperatures could get quite warm, time spent out of doors would have been prized for its relaxation and for the chance to enjoy the sublime beauty of nature. Being outdoors naturally afforded the opportunity for taking walks whether in a garden or in wide, open spaces. Elizabeth Bennett demonstrated that even with a muddy petticoat, walking presented the perfect opportunity to enjoy the outdoors. As Emma admires the beauty of Donwell Abbey she says, "It was a sweet view -- sweet to the eye and the mind. English verdure, English culture, English comfort, seen under a sun bright, without being oppressive." (*Emma*, Chp. 42)

Berries! Fresh berries! Can you guess another popular activity in summertime England? That's right. Picking strawberries! Mr. Knightley planned a delightful afternoon for his friends to pick strawberries at Donwell Abbey. Mr. Knightley, of course, was the perfect host, and Mrs. Elton certainly knew her strawberries even though they would have been very different from the larger berries of today.

Jane Austen, through Mrs. Elton, tells us about the variety of strawberries available in England at the start of the 19th century. "The best fruit in England — every body's favourite — always wholesome. These the finest beds and finest sorts. — Delightful to gather for one's self — the only way of really enjoying them. Morning decidedly the best time — never tired — every sort good — hautboy infinitely superior — no comparison — the others hardly eatable — hautboys very scarce — Chili preferred — white wood finest flavour of all — price of strawberries in London — abundance about Bristol — Maple Grove — cultivation — beds when to be renewed — gardeners thinking exactly different — no general rule — gardeners never to be put out of their way — delicious fruit — only too rich to be eaten much of — inferior to cherries — currants more refreshing — only objection to gathering strawberries the stooping — glaring sun — tired to death — could bear it no longer — must go and sit in the shade." (*Emma*, Chp. 42)

Dear Mrs. Elton.

Jane Austen enjoyed strawberries herself. She enjoyed eating them and the gathering of the fresh fruit as she tells Cassandra in one letter dated in June 1808, "I want to hear of your gathering Strawberries, we have had them three times together here."

What better way to combine time outdoors with the enjoyable activity of eating than with a picnic? And as for location, how about a spot with scenic views like Box Hill? It can't get much better! Jane Austen used the picnic on Box Hill to effectively further her plot around Emma and her companions while they enjoyed a delicious picnic and a

beautiful warm afternoon on Box Hill. As Jane Austen tells us of Emma and the group picnicking at Box Hill, "They had a very fine day for Box Hill; and all the other outward circumstances of arrangement, accommodation, and punctuality, were in favour of a pleasant party... Seven miles were travelled in expectation of enjoyment, and everybody had a burst of admiration on first arriving;" (*Emma*, Chp. 43)

Picnic at Box Hill
Himmapaan N. Puttapipat

Even though the heat of the summer months could be uncomfortable in Regency England, its occupants knew how to make the most of where they were and enjoy the beautiful countryside diversions at their disposal. Whether taking a walk, picking strawberries or partaking of a delicious picnic meal, the outdoors offered a pleasurable opportunity to enjoy the beautiful outdoors of God's creation. What a delightful way to spend a hot summer month. But there's even more ahead! Let's make our way to August.

August

A Crescendo: from Seeding to Growth to Harvest

"-- in summer there is dust, and in winter there is dirt."
Mrs. Elton to Mr. Knightley ~ *Emma*

LLAMAS DAY

THE DRY, BREATHLESS HEAT of summer has settled over the harvest fields. The summer has reached its peak and with it comes the celebration of Llamas Day on August 1st. Llamas Day marks the turning point in the year from the growing season to the harvest season. It celebrates the crops that have been planted, nourished and have now grown to the time of their harvesting. Llamas Day, also known as Loaf Day, is the first festival to celebrate the impending harvest season.

The term, Loaf Day, comes from the baking of bread from the first wheat harvested of the year. The freshly-harvested wheat is ground into new grain and tradition has that the baking of the loaves tests the worthiness of the season's first crop. It was the custom to bring these loaves, made from the first fruits of the harvest, to church for blessing. It was also customary in the rural and pastoral parts of England that tenants were compelled to bring newly-harvested wheat to their landlords on or before the first day of

August in recognition of Llamas Day.

In ancient practices, the first wheat loaf was broken into four pieces and a piece left in each corner of the barn. The four pieces were thought to magically bring protection to the harvest bounty stored within.

Even though neither Llamas Day or Loaf Day are specifically mentioned in Jane Austen's six novels, it was a holiday certainly celebrated during the Regency Era as a continuation of long-held, ancient customs. After our visit to August, let's move on to September which brings with it the hope of some cooler temperatures.

September

Angelic Warrior, Protector Against the Night

"Michaelmas came; and now Anne's heart must be in Kellynch again."
Anne Elliott ~ Persuasion

IN THE MONTH OF September, Michaelmas Day is celebrated on the 29th. Michaelmas Day is a shortened term for St. Michael's Mass which is how it had been known and celebrated in the Middle Ages. It is also the last day of the harvest season that began on August 1st, Llamas Day.

The holiday is named for the arch angel, Michael, who was one of heaven's principle angelic warriors. He was the protector of the night and the arch angel who drove Satan and his evil minions from heaven. Michael is mentioned seven times in scripture, each time as a heavenly entity and warlike figure. One

San Michele il drago
Raffaelo Sanzio

verse of the Bible describes Michael in Daniel 12:1 as "... Michael, the great prince who protects your people..."

As weather turns cooler and days grow shorter at the end of harvest season, St. Michael's defenses were called upon to ward off negative forces which were thought to grow stronger with the increasing darkness. With the hint of the winter coming, Michaelmas was also when the night curfew began. The night curfew was marked by the ringing of the church bell, usually at 9:00 p.m., and the bell was rung once for each month of the year that had passed.

Michaelmas is considered one of the quarter days of the year and a day when rents were due, laborers were hired and leases begun. In *Pride & Prejudice*, Mrs. Bennett has heard that Netherfield was to be "let at last" and Mr. Bingley, "was to take possession before Michaelmas, . . . " (Chp. 1) and in *Persuasion*, when Kellynch was to be let to the Crofts, Jane Austen says, "The Crofts were to have possession at Michaelmas; and as Sir Walter proposed removing to Bath in the course of the preceding month, there was no time to be lost." (Chp. 5) Michaelmas was also a time debts were to be paid, magistrates and officials elected and the beginning of school terms at universities.

Goose was a prominent feature at the Michaelmas feast. How did it come to figure into the festivities on Michaelmas? There are a couple of interesting accounts. One account says Queen Elizabeth I was eating goose when she received word of the defeat of the Armada. She said that in recognition, goose should be eaten on Michaelmas in celebration. A second theory has to do with the celebration of the quarter day when rents and bills were due. Tenants would often bring a goose to their landlord in hopes of possibly delaying their rent payment for awhile. In favor

of this prospect, geese were thought to be very tasty at this time of year.

Since Michaelmas was also known as Goose Day, it is of no matter the exact reason, but goose was certainly the highly-anticipated feature for the meal of the day. A goose, fattened off stubble from the harvest fields, was traditionally eaten to protect against financial ruin. Superstition of the day held that if you ate goose on Michaelmas Day, you would certainly not lack for money in the coming year. As the saying goes:

> *"Eat a goose on Michaelmas Day,*
> *Want not for money all the year."*

Jane Austen certainly subscribed to this superstition as she wrote in a letter to her sister, Cassandra, "I dined upon goose yesterday – which I hope will secure a good sale of my second edition."

The goose was also thought to be good for weather forecasting. If the breast bone of the cooked goose was brown, the coming winter would be mild. But if the bones were white or slightly blue, the coming winter would be severe.

Michaelmas Day was at one time celebrated on October 10th, and known as "Old Michaelmas Day." British folklore says that Old Michaelmas Day was the last day blackberries should be

picked. But why? The story goes that this was the day Michael kicked the devil out of heaven. When the devil landed on earth, he landed right on a blackberry bush. He was so mad, he cursed the fruit, charred the bush with fire, spat on it and then stomped the berries to make sure the berries were unfit for eating or using in any way. It is still advised not to eat blackberries after September 29th so a Michaelmas pie is made from the last berries of the season.

Well, we've enjoyed our goose dinner and blackberry pie and now it's time to move into Michaelmas Term which is the final Term of the year and starts in October. The weather is turning cooler so be sure to wear your pelisse. Step lively - we're heading into the time of year when festivals and holidays truly abound.

October

---❖---

A New Year is Stitched to the Old

*"Soul, Soul for a Souling cake, I pray good missus, a
Souling Cake; Apple or pear, a plum or a cherry; anything good thing to
make us all merry."*

Celtic Soul Caker's Song

I T ALL BEGAN *AND* ended on Samhain; the end of summer
and the beginning of winter, the end of an old year
and the start of a new. Samhain is an ancient term
literally meaning "The End of Summer," and festivities began with a harvest festival, marking the end of the harvest
season and signaling
the start of the cold,
barrenness of winter.
On Samhain, fires in
each home hearth

were extinguished and embers from a village bonfire were
gathered to start the home hearth fires anew. This ancient
ritual symbolized a fresh start to a new year with hope and
prosperity for the year to come. It was also believed that
the bright light from the bonfires kept some of the evil
spirits away who were thought to wander that night and
also helped to light the way for souls coming to earth from
Purgatory.

Even though the Samhain festival itself was recognized
November 1st, actual celebrations kicked off the evening

before on October 31st. All Hallow's Eve, known to be one of the ghostliest nights of the year, was eventually changed to All Hallows Even, root for Hallowe'en or what we know today as Halloween. With the old year waning and the new year beginning, this was believed to be a time when "a new year was being stitched to the old" and the lines between the present world and the spirit world blurred. Because of these beliefs, October 31st was a highly superstitious night.

Witches and other evil creatures were thought to roam the earth on this night, and the door from the supernatural world was believed to be opened so souls who had died with unfinished business could return to earth to complete their work. Country folk would leave doors and windows unlocked to welcome these spirits from the other world whether that meant inviting them to partake in festivities or to warm themselves at the hearth.

The poor and needy wandered the village chanting a rhyme much like the ancient Soul Cakers song, "Soul, Soul for a Souling Cake, I pray good missus, a Souling Cake; Apple or pear, a plum or a cherry, anything good thing to make us all merry." A Souling Cake was typically a flat round bun made from oat flour. It doesn't sound very enticing until you add some juicy, sweet fruit which made it a desired favorite. The tradition of chanting

A soul-cake! A soul-cake!
Please good Missis, a soul cake!
An apple, a pear, a plum or a cherry,
Any good thing to make us all merry.
One for Peter, two for Paul
Three for Him who made us all.

SOUL CAKES

Forages and Finds

a rhyme for a sweet treat evolved into what was called "beggar's night" which in turn became "trick or treat." Tradition says that if you handed out a "treat," good fortune would come to your house the next year. However, if you didn't comply, "beggar's night" could turn into "mischief night" and you might awake in the morning to find a "trick" had been played on you. Mischief and lawlessness were given free reign so you might just find your cow in a far-off pasture, a gate unlocked, or your garden destroyed.

On Hallow's Eve, homes were lit by rustic lanterns carved from beets, rutabagas or turnips which were known then as "neeps." Even though we are familiar with carved pumpkins today, pumpkins weren't used in England until later when they were brought to Europe from the American new world. These glowing lanterns were set out in the hope of welcoming home friendly souls while at the same time, chasing away evil spirits wandering that night. One of those wandering spirits might be "Stingy Jack."

Stingy Jack, so the legend goes, was an astute farmer who somehow managed to trick the old devil into a tree. He wouldn't let the devil come down until the devil

Stingy Jack
Jovan Ukropina

agreed he would never let Jack into hell. The story says that when Jack died, he was too sinful to enter heaven and the

devil wouldn't let him into hell so he had nowhere to go. He carved a lantern out of a turnip, put a candle inside, and used it to light his way as he wandered the earth looking for a resting place. He became known as "Jack of the Lantern," later shortened to "jack-o-lantern."

Since the dead were thought to be roaming this night, the living who didn't want to encounter these wandering souls, painted their faces or wore masks and disguises in hopes of preventing the deceased's spirits from recognizing them.

Even though Samhain, also known as Halloween, could be a fearsome night, it didn't stop residents from enjoying fun activities that promised the opportunity to meet other people from outside their village. Some of these traditions have been passed down through the decades and are still enjoyed today. During the festival celebration on Hallow's Eve, young people would bob for apples floating in water or attempt taking a bite of an apple on a string. The old wives' tale goes that whoever was able to take the first bite from the apple would be the first to marry in the new year. Today, bobbing for apples is still enjoyed at fall festivals and parties, but now it's most often a fun way to get wet or get someone else wet. Of course, there's always the outside hope of actually hemming up an apple and taking a bite.

Nut Crack Night was another fun Regency custom on Hallow's Eve. Hoping to learn the name of a future mate, some young hopeful threw two hazelnuts into an open fire one named for themself and one named for the person their heart desired. The person throwing the nuts into the fire would then recite, "If you hate me, spite and fly. If you

love me, burn awa." If the
nuts burned side by side,
the two were meant to be
together. If though the nuts
flew apart, sorry, the two
were meant to be apart.

Did Jane Austen ever
bob for apples or throw acorns into the fire? Being the
daughter of a clergyman, it's highly doubtful she would
have participated in Hallow's Eve activities but akin to
this night of mischief, she did love a good mystery. Austen
demonstrated knowledge of the gothic novels so popular
during her time with particular familiarity of Anne Rad-
cliffe's, *The Mysteries of Udolpho.* With sparkling humor,
she caricatured the gothic novels with several references
in Austen's *Northanger Abbey.* Other books written around
the time of Jane Austen are even more closely associated
with modern day Halloween celebrations such as *Franken-
stein* and *The Legend of Sleepy Hollow.* Austen may not have
actively participated in the Hallow's Eve festivities of her
time, but she vividly drew on events she possibly came to
know from friends in the village but most especially from
what she experienced vicariously through her own reading which became central to *Northanger Abbey*'s charm.

What a hauntingly mysterious month October has
turned out to be. So many things to tease the imagination!
It's time to continue our holiday journey though so let's
leave our masks and jack-o-lanterns behind, take a bite or
two out of the apple we "bobbed" for, and see what lies in
wait among November's festivals and celebrations.

November

—※·≍·※—

Saints, Souls, Schemes and a Soldier

"His Martinmas will come; as it does to every good hog . . ."
Old English Saying

THE HAUNTING CELEBRATIONS OF Hallow's Eve were a prelude to All Saints Day on November 1st, quickly followed by All Souls Day on November 2nd. Why two holidays days so close together? Their names are similar but are they alike or are they distinctly different? Let's take a closer look to see.

ALL SAINTS DAY

IN A REIGN OF terror during the early years of the Christian church, the Roman Empire martyred Christians for their faith. Their methods were cruel and those who died suffered greatly. These martyrs who died in defense of their beliefs, have been honored and recognized by the church for hundreds of years. In 607 CE, the Byzantine Emperor Phocas made a gift of the beautiful Roman Pantheon to the church's pope. After removing statutes of the Roman gods, the Pantheon was sanctified to be to "all saints" who had died from the Roman persecution

the first 300 years of the church's existence. Unfortunately, the Romans were quite zealous in their executions and there were too many martyred saints to allow a separate day of recognition for each. As a remedy, all were grouped together and celebrated in one accord on All Saints Day.

November 1st evolved as the date to celebrate All Saints Day originating with Pope Gregory III's dedication of St Peter's Basilica on that date sometime between 731 and 741CE. Only a short hundred years later in 875, Pope Gregory IV asked King Louis the Pious to proclaim November 1st, as All Saints Day throughout the Roman Empire. All Saints Day was a "modernized" term for what had been known as All Hallow's Day. Remember All Hallow's Eve celebrated the night before? Hallow was a fitting term to honor martyred saints meaning "holy" or "sacred."

ALL SOULS DAY

ALL SOULS DAY, NOVEMBER 2nd, was a date set aside to recognize departed souls of all those of faith whether martyrs or otherwise. Prayers were offered and candles lit in churches on behalf of souls from all denominations including the Church of England. The *Book of Common Prayer* contains this verse still recited today regarding All Saints Day: "God who hast knit together thine elect in one communion and fellowship, in the mystical body of thy Son Christ our Lord; Grant us grace so to follow thy blessed Saints in all virtuous and godly living..."

GUY FAWKES DAY

FROM SAINTS TO THE dastardly Guy Fawkes. Guy Fawkes Day is celebrated November 5th today just as it was celebrated starting in 1605. What did Guy Fawkes do to garner such infamy and long-lasting recognition?

In the years leading up to 1605, Catholics in England were feeling mistreated and not granted the same level of treatment as members of the Church of England. To rally fellow Catholics to their side and bring recognition to their plight, Guy Fawkes and a dedicated band of twelve co-conspirators, plotted to blow up King James I and Parliament on November 5th, the opening day of the Parliamentary session in 1605. The scheme came to be known as "The Gun Powder Plot." In the cellar far below the Parliament chambers, the schemers placed over 36 barrels of black gun powder (almost two tons!) in hopes of inflicting as much damage as possible on the building and its occupants. Unfortunately for Guy Fawkes, but fortunately for King James and Parliament, Fawkes, the gun powder specialist, was caught lurking in the cellar area with incriminating matches in his pocket. Legend says a letter from an anonymous writer gave warning to the group's nefarious activities thus thwarting the conspiracy. Fawkes was sent to the Tower of London where he was tortured and summarily executed. His fellow planners were all eventually caught or killed outright.

Guy Fawkes Monochrome Engraving

King James I, in conjunction with Parliament, declared an annual day of celebration be held in recognition of the "joyful day of deliverance." Annual celebrations have been held ever since with the lighting of fireworks, bon fires and the burning of Guy Fawkes in effigy. It is still tradition today that on the first day of a new session of Parliament, a ceremonial searching of a cellar (the cellar from 1605 no longer exists) be done by the Yeoman of the Guard.

Did Jane Austen celebrate Guy Fawkes' Day? An interesting thought to ponder. Even though the holiday isn't mentioned in her novels or letters, it would certainly be logical to assume she would have enjoyed a bon fire or watched a fireworks display with her family to celebrate the "joyful deliverance" of the English government and monarchy from a group of rebels.

MARTINMAS

ST. MARTIN OF TOURS was, originally, a dedicated fourth century Roman soldier, but a dream changed his destiny forever. While traveling by horseback one day, he encountered a poor beggar at the city gates of Amiens. Having compassion on the poor man, Martin cut his red woolen cloak in two with his sword and gave a portion to the poor man. The next night in a dream, Martin saw Christ wearing the red cloak surrounded by angels. In the dream, the Lord asked Martin if he recognized the cloak which, of course, he did.

St. Martin of deTours
Courtesy of eluminure

Because of the dream, Martin then realized the need to dedicate his life to the Lord. The remnant of the cloak, or cappa in Latin, kept by Martin became a highly-revered relic. The building where it was preserved became known as cappella, the root word for our chapel and chaplain.

Roman Emperor Julian declared Martin a coward and placed him in prison. After Martin declared himself a soldier of Christ rather than of Rome, it would not be lawful for him to fight any longer. Even though Julian had him imprisoned, he was later released.

Martin's quiet life of dedication and service became known and even though he didn't seek higher office and even actively avoided it, he was tricked into coming to the

city of Tours under the ruse of a wealthy man's sick wife needing him. Totally unaware of the trickery, Martin traveled to Tours immediately. Hardly had he arrived when the local officials declared him Bishop of the Church of Tours by popular acclamation. Martin was less than pleased and rather than be installed as Bishop, he hid in a goose pen. Legend tells the inglorious tale of Martin's hiding place being discovered due to the cackling of the infringed-upon geese. Even though he didn't seek the role, Martin did serve and led an exemplary life as Bishop.

The Feast of Martinmas is celebrated on November 11th, coming at the end of autumn and celebrating the time of harvest which brings full barns and stocked pantries ready for the cold winter ahead. Preparations for winter also meant the time to butcher animals thus engaging the old English saying, "His Martinmas will come as it does to every good hog" which means "he will get his comeuppance."

On the day of the celebration, individuals attended Mass but then spent the rest of the day enjoying games, parades through the village, dances and a large feast. The

celebration banquet itself was, much like our own Thanksgiving meal but rather than turkey, the Martinmas celebration centered around a golden brown "Martin's goose." "Saint Martin's wine" made from grapes of the recent harvest was also enjoyed at the feast.

symbolically or literally, on the religious aspect of the holiday. The Christmastide season reflected on the religious aspects of the holiday, but the season was also a time to focus on family and friends.

The English countryside's provincial villages and country homes were far from dreary during the dark, cold nights of winter as joys of the festive season began to fill the air. But was this just in provincial villages and country homes? What about the larger cities and towns? Didn't they celebrate the Christmas season? An interesting question and an even more interesting answer. How or even if you celebrated Christmas actually depended on where you lived. Agricultural villages and large country houses enjoyed the festivities of the season while those living in London or larger towns saw Christmas customs as rustic or unfashionable. It wasn't until Charles Dicken's *A Christmas Carol* was published in 1846, that city dwellers got into the Christmas spirit. But, let's take a step back and take a closer look at how Jane Austen and her family might have celebrated this significant and merry season.

STIR IT UP SUNDAY

HOLIDAY FESTIVITIES BEGAN WITH the making of the traditional Christmas pudding. On the fourth Sunday before Christmas, the whole family gathered in the kitchen and everyone participated in the annual tradition of "stirring up" and steaming the pudding that would be served on Christmas Day. Christmas

Puddings, Pantomimes and So Much More

"Wassaile the trees, that they may beare
You many a Plum and many a Peare;
For more or less fruits they will bring,
As you do give them Wassailing"
Old English Rhyme

IT'S DECEMBER AND THAT means it's time for Christmas! What did Christmas mean for Regency Era dwellers? Did they have presents under a Christmas tree, sing carols in the village square, bustle about doing a flurry of shopping and attend lovely parties and elegant balls? The answer is yes . . . and no. Christmas during the Regency Era had a much different focus than Christmas today so let's explore the fun and traditions of a lively Christmastide season in Regency England.

By the time of the Regency Era, Christmas was slowly regaining its observation. In the 1640s, England's Commonwealth Parliament passed measures to seriously curtail or even ban practices of the season altogether. The Puritans who were in power at the time considered the holiday's observances raucous and inappropriate for what was supposed to be a holy season. When the monarchy returned to power, and in due time, the ban was lifted, but celebrations were slow to resume. Even when observances began again, they were subdued and focused, whether

Just like its harvest's barns, November is stocked full of interesting and meaningful holidays. But, there's just one more month to go and our holiday journey will be complete. It's time to join the Yuletide festivities of December.

puddings of the time had to be aged before serving so they were made well in advance to be ready for the big day. The name "Stir Up Sunday" doesn't actually come from stirring the pudding on that day but rather from a scripture in the *Book of Common Prayer* of 1549 to be quoted on that day and which states: "Stir up, we beseech thee, O Lord, the wills of thy faithful people; that they, plenteously bringing forth the fruit of good works, may of thee be plenteously be rewarded; through Jesus Christ our Lord. Amen."

Tradition and symbolism abound in the pudding's preparation. The recipe for the traditional Christmas pudding called for 13 ingredients, symbolic of Christ and His twelve apostles. Each family member took a turn stirring which also had a practical side since stirring was actually hard work. A special wooden spoon was to be used in recognition of the crib and stable where Christ was born. Each stirrer stirred the pudding clockwise, or from east to west, in remembrance of the journey of the magi. The stirrer was to make a secret wish while stirring keeping

Christmas Pudding
WordPress

their eyes closed tight. After everyone had had their turn, tiny charms or silver coins were added to the pudding. Upon their discovery on Christmas Day, the finder would have good fortune in the coming year. Today, silver coins are placed *beneath* the serving of pudding to prevent unwanted visits to the dentist.

ADVENT

ADVENT COMES FROM THE Latin term, *adventus* which means "coming." It was and is observed the four weeks and four Sundays before Christmas and is a time to quietly turn thoughts and contemplation toward the birth of Christ while preparing thoughts and hearts for His second coming.

During the Regency Era, and times before and after, Advent was recognized and celebrated with candles or in some countries, wreaths, bedecked with small gifts. One gift on the wreath was to be selected and opened on each day of the Advent period. Still popular are advent calendars with small windows, one to be opened each day of Advent revealing a small picture inside representing the season. Advent calendars began with the use of images related to the Christmas holidays, but today there are advent calendars of every type and themed toward everything imaginable.

ST. NICHOLAS DAY

LET THE FESTIVITIES BEGIN! December 6th, St. Nicholas' Day, was the official beginning of the holiday season and the day seasonal activities started in earnest. Small gifts might be exchanged on this day but the focus was primarily on gifts for the children. Adults rarely took part in an exchange. On this day, families, friends and

relatives began a round of holiday visits, some with extended stays, that brought loved ones together for a variety of social activities. There were parties for card-playing, ice skating, dining and of course, lavish balls all held for the enjoyment of holiday guests of all ages. No matter the type of gathering for the holiday, each one enhanced the festive air of the joyous season.

CHRISTMAS EVE AND CHRISTMAS DAY

WHILE BASIC PREPARATIONS MAY have begun earlier in the month including making the Christmas pudding, and while family and friends exchange visits during the month of December, the crescendo of the season reaches its peak on Christmas Eve. Greens have been gathered from the fields and family and friends gather to hang the holly, ivy, hellebore (a Christmas rose), and of course, mistletoe, throughout the house. If you lived in an area where mistletoe didn't grow, kindly friends

or relatives might send some to you via a mail coach. Greens were not gathered and definitely not brought into the house until Christmas Eve. If they were brought in the house any earlier, it could mean bad luck for the household in the coming year. The mistletoe would probably have been fashioned into what

glorious eye of the room." (by a contributor to the *New Monthly Magazine,* December 1, 1825).

Jane Austen certainly agreed with the importance of the Yule log fire as she made it the centerpiece of a scene at Uppercross in Chapter 14 of *Persuasion,* "On one side was a table occupied by some chattering girls cutting up silk and gold paper and on the other were trestles and trays, bending under the weight of brawn and cold pies where riotous boys were holding high revel; the whole completed by a roaring Christmas fire which seemed determined to be heard in spite of the noise of the others."

YULE CANDLE

AT THE END OF the 18th century, it became a custom for chandlers (candlemakers) to make a gift of a Yule candle to their regular customers. The Yule candle was a very large candle lit at sunset on Christmas Eve and was to burn until Christmas Day service or dawn of Christmas Day. It was also supposed to burn on each of the twelve nights of the Christmastide season between Christmas and Epiphany. The glow of the Yule candle was believed to convey special blessings to anyone or anything touched by its glow. Christmas Eve supper was served by its light while holiday breads were placed nearby to be kept fresh. Precious possessions were also placed within reach of its glow for safekeeping.

A WASSAILING

AS FAMILY AND FRIENDS gather on Christmas Eve, they might be found sipping a cup of steaming hot wassail. While wassail certainly sounds like something "Christmasy," what exactly is wassail and why did drinking this steaming beverage become a significant part of Christmas Eve tradition?

Throughout history, wassailing has actually had two different connotations. The first is an old English term *waes hael* which means "be well." At the beginning of the year, subjects of the Lord of the Manor would come together. The Lord would then call out *waes hael*. The crowd would answer him back, "drink hael" or "drink and be healthy."

In other parts of England, wassailers carried a bowl full of spiced ale as they went door to door singing, drinking and bidding everyone they met good health in the coming year. Those the wassailers called upon would give the singers some drink, money or Christmas food. The traditional day for wassailing had long been Twelfth Night. Over time as the calendar was aligned with the solar year, the start of a new year became January 1st and wassailing became part of Christmas Eve celebrations.

In cider-producing regions, another form of "wassailing" was held where large pans or buckets filled with cider and roasted apples were carried to the apple orchard after supper on Twelfth Night. Everyone gathered would sing "a wassailing" song in a custom that came to be known as "wassailing of the trees." The song was sung

as a petition for growth and fruit aplenty much like this wassailing rhyme:

> *"Health to thee, good apple-tree,*
> *Well to bear, pocket-fulls, hat-fulls,*
> *Peck-fulls, bushel-bag fulls."*

At the conclusion of the song, all would take a drink of cider from their cup and throw the rest at the apple trees to insure health and plentiful fruit in the coming year.

The term "wassailing" encompasses both the practice of singing door to door and singing traditional songs to fruit trees for a plentiful harvest in the coming year. No matter whether it be Twelfth Night or Christmas Eve, sipping wassail from a punch cup or "a-wassailing" the local trees, family and friends are brought together in merry comradeship.

Wassail Bowl

INGREDIENTS:

4 cups apple cider
1/8 teaspoon ground allspice
1 tablespoon orange liqueur
¼ teaspoon cinnamon
¼ teaspoon ground cloves
1/8 teaspoon ground allspice
1/2 cup firmly packed dark brown sugar
Salt to Taste
1/2 cup dark rum
½ lemon, thinly sliced
1/4 cup brandy
½ orange, thinly sliced
Whipped cream
Freshly grated nutmeg
1 tablespoon orange liqueur

DIRECTIONS:

In a saucepan bring the apple cider to a boil over medium heat, add the brown sugar and cook mixture, stirring, until the sugar is dissolved. Remove pan from heat and add the rum, brandy, orange liqueur, cinnamon, cloves,

allspice, salt, and fruit slices. Heat mixture over moderate heat, stirring, 2 minutes. Pour the wassail into wine glasses and top it with whipped cream and freshly grated nutmeg.

La Belle Cuisine, Recipe from the Gourmet Archives

MUMMERS

C HRISTMAS EVE IS PACKED full of fun traditions one of which is the appearance of travelling actors known as mummers. Mummers wander the streets on Christmas Eve dressed in outrageously bright and colorful costumes asking if "mummers" were wanted. "Mummer" or "disguised person" if called upon, would perform brief plays ending with a song and a collection of coins. These colorful characters were troops of all male actors with a history reaching back to the late 1200s. Mummers sometimes perform on the street but most typically perform in homes or pubs. Still active today, mummers participate in parades and other activities associated with various holidays including Christmas, Easter and sometimes, but rarely, Halloween and All Souls Day.

CHRISTMAS PANTOMIMES

P ANTOMIME IS A FASCINATINGLY British tradition with the word literally meaning "all kinds of mime." Pantomime has been a part of the English Christmastide season for hundreds of years with plays that include

embellished acting, role reversals between men and women and slap stick comedy all topped off with audience participation. Despite the name, these performances are very verbal, being written and performed at two levels, one for children and one for adults. While the children enjoy a familiar fairy tale plot and the slapstick comedy, the words, innuendos and political barbs are aimed at the adults in the audience.

Pantomimes are plays typically based on well-known children's stories such as "Cinderella," "Peter Pan," "Sleeping Beauty," and so on. Men play the women's roles while women, of course, then play the men. The audience has a role too whether it's to boo the dastardly villain, tell the wicked queen she really *is not* the fairest of them all or to call out a warning to the fair damsel when a scoundrel is sneaking up behind. Slapstick comedy is an important factor of the pantomime for how else would those ugly step sisters get the custard pies in the face they so richly deserve? By the end of the raucous performance and holding true to the fairy tale upon which the story is based, the mean old villain is defeated, the hero and heroine fall madly in love, and everyone lives happily ever after.

Pantomimes were performed across England from the best theatres in London all the way to the tiny village assembly halls. A pantomime might be a lavish production or it might be a home-grown performance making do with what is on hand. No matter the style or location, pantomimes, as an ongoing part of British Christmas tradition, have always been well attended.

Christmas pantomime performances are still popular

today, hundreds of years after their beginnings in the early masques begun during the Elizabethan and Stuart period. William Makepeace Thackeray, makes mention of the popularity of pantomimes in *Round About the Christmas Tree*, "Very few men in the course of nature can expect to see all the pantomimes in one season, but I hope to the end of my life I shall never forego reading about them in that delicious sheet of the *Times* which appears on the morning after Boxing Day."

CHRISTMAS DAY

AFTER THE CELEBRATORY FESTIVITIES of Christmas Eve, Christmas Day observances are much more sedate in nature. Everyone is up bright and early to attend Christmas Day service and then gather for the much-anticipated Christmas feast. The feast, more than a month in the making, consists of holiday favorites and delicacies served once a year, especially for this occasion.

The main dish, until the 17th century, was the head of a boar. Boars were wild hogs and were fearsome creatures who throughout English history were thought to be the most formidable animals in the forest. The boar's head on the Christmas feast table symbolized good's victory over evil and Christ's triumph over the devil. Boar became extinct in England in 1185, so the head of a pig was substituted instead. As accompaniment to the pig's head on the table for the main course, roast goose and turkey were included. Turkeys weren't enjoyed until after 1550 when

they were brought to England from the New World. Side dishes for the meal included stuffing for the turkey and vegetables such as potatoes, squash, carrots and brussel sprouts.

A wealthy family having Christmas dinner.

A variety of delectable desserts served as the grand finale to the meal. One such dessert was marchpane or what we today call marzipan. Marzipan is a confectionary item made primarily of sugar (or honey) and almond meal (ground almonds). Almond oil or another type of oil extract can be added for more flavor. Marzipan was commonly rolled into thin sheets and used as a glaze for icing on special cakes such as wedding cakes, birthday cakes and in this instance, the cake served for Christmas dinner dessert. It is particularly common in the United Kingdom for a thin sheet of marzipan to be placed on top of large fruitcakes.

Over four weeks ago, the family came together on Stir It Up Sunday and worked together to make Plum Pudding, England's most cherished Christmas dessert. Even though the name Plum Pudding dates back to the 1670s, by the Regency Era, the pudding no longer contained plums, they had been replaced by raisins and currants. This famous pudding is also the famous "figgy" pudding from the Christmas carol, *We Wish You a Merry Christmas*. Interestingly though, the pudding doesn't contain figs either. Whether containing plums, figs, raisins, or currants,

plum pudding was considered a necessity for a truly English Christmas.

Serving the Christmas Pudding
Austenprose

So, after being steamed and hung in a cheesecloth for four weeks, the pudding's moment of glory comes when it is placed on a festive plate and doused with brandy. A sprig of holly is placed on top to represent the crown of thorns worn by Christ at the crucifixion. As the climax of the Christmas feast, the pudding is set ablaze before being served to delighted guests.

Following such a festive meal, this might seem the time to exchange gifts. However, during the Regency Era, a small token or gift might have been given to the children, but that would be the extent of the exchange. Rather, Christmas was used as a time to focus on those in need or those in a lower social economic class. Landowners were expected to show generosity by entertaining their tenants and neighbors. Many landowners held a party much like an open house and for the poorer members of the community, this was their *only* holiday celebration. Regency Era inhabitants took seriously the obligation to help their neighbors and those less fortunate as this is the very definition of the Regency Christmastide season.

BOXING DAY

ECEMBER 26TH, KNOWN AS Boxing Day or as St. Stephen's Day, continues the Christmas theme of sharing with the needy and less fortunate. Traditionally on this day, the landowner gentry, employers, and so on, would give gifts to servants and tradesmen to thank them for their good service throughout the year. These gifts were packaged in boxes for easy transport which resulted in the day becoming known as Boxing Day. The observance originated in an ancient practice of giving money or sturdy household wares to those of lower classes.

As part of the Christmas tradition in Regency England and during Jane Austen's time, those living on large country estates including the landowner, servants, tenants, and villagers, all came together this one time of year at Christmas. This gathering presented a timely opportunity for the landowner to distribute his annual stipend of goods and necessities for the coming year. So, on December 26th, the day after Christmas Day, everyone came together to receive their box of goods which might contain such things as spun cloth, staple food items, candles and other housewares needed in the coming year. To make everything easier to transport, boxes were used to carry their supplies back to their respective homes thus accounting for another reason the day was called Boxing Day.

Another possible origin of Boxing Day holds that on the day after Christmas Day, employees would bring boxes with them to work. Employers would place coins in the

box as their gift at the end of the year for good service. Another similar possibility says employers would give each servant a small clay-type box on December 26th. The recipients would then smash open the box to retrieve the cash left inside just for them.

A religious version of the Boxing Day name claims that alms boxes left in the church for holiday donations for the poor were opened on Christmas Day. Donations were then distributed by the clergy on the next day, December 26th. The name then, according to this account, originates from a church lock box.

No matter the origin of Boxing Day, its common characteristic is giving funds or functional goods to the needy such as those in a lower social class or faithful servants whose service is valued and appreciated. Whether its smashing earthenware boxes, dropping coins in a church alms box or landowners handing boxes of supplies to servants and tenants, the day meant people looking out for and taking care of those less fortunate than themselves. The focus of the day was to give to those in need without a lavish gift exchange between those who already had plenty.

JANUARY - THE END AND BACK TO THE BEGINNING; THE HOLIDAY CELEBRATION CULMINATION

AS WE LEARNED ABOUT January when we started twelve months ago, the Christmastide season culminates every year with the celebration of epiphany, also

known as Twelfth Night. The celebration comes every January 5th, the Eve of Epiphany, and Epiphany Day, January 6th. There are twelve days between Christmas Day and January 6th and a popular holiday song, *The Twelve Days of Christmas*, had some logically-specu-

Twelve Days of Christmas Song
Wikipedia

lating people thinking it was written with this time period in mind. It could have originally been a rhyming limerick played as part of a "mischief and forfeits" game.

This was a heady, festive time when young lovers were looking for ways to woo the other throughout the hectic social activity of the holiday season. Jane Austen herself felt the tug of young love during this fanciful holiday social season. She writes her sister, Cassandra, on January 9th, 1796, to tell her about the Manydown Ball she'd attended and where she most likely had met and danced with Tom LeFroy. At the Ball, she tells Cassandra, "Imagine to yourself everything most profligate and shocking in the way of dancing and sitting down together. I can expose myself however, only once more, because he leaves the country soon after next Friday, on which day we are to have a dance at Ashe after all." A romantic but fateful interlude as they were not destined to be together again.

In spite of the cold and snow classically associated with the Christmastide season, weather at this time of year in Regency England was typically warm and balmy. In a

letter to Cassandra in December 1815, Jane Austen wrote of the weather, "I am sorry my mother has been suffering, and am afraid this exquisite weather is too good to agree with her I enjoy it all over me, from toe to toe, from right to left, longitudinally, perpendicularly, diagonally; and I cannot but selfishly hope we are to have it last till Christmas – nice unwholesome, unseasonable, relaxing, close, muggy weather." Such weather provided ample opportunity for revelers to enjoy an Epiphany full of parties, celebrations and a ball to climax the day.

This festive day was filled with an abundance of games including whist, bullet pudding, charades and snap dragon. While we might be more familiar with the card game of whist, the games of bullet pudding, charades, and snap dragon were popular to play most especially during the Christmastide season.

Bullet pudding was an intense game of delicate skill. Jane Austen's niece, Fanny Austen Knight, describes a characteristic game of Bullet Pudding in a letter to a Miss Chapman with: "I was surprised that you did not know what a Bullet Pudding is but as you don't I will endeavor to describe it as follows: You must have a large pewter dish filled with flour which you must pile up into a sort of pudding with a peak at the top, you must then lay a Bullet at the top & everybody cuts a slice of it & the person that is cutting it when the Bullet falls must poke about with their nose & chins till they find it & then take it out with their mouths which makes them strange figures a covered with flour but the worst is that you must not laugh for fear of the flour getting up your nose & mouth & choking you.

You must not use your hands in taking the bullet out."

Charades were also a popular diversion in the Regency Era but different from how we define charades today. During the Regency Era, charades were written verses with clever hints to a particular word. Jane Austen was quite proficient in writing charades. Check out the two below attributed to her writing and see if you can ascertain the word being described in the verse.

When my first is a task to a young girl of spirit,
And my second confines her to finish the piece
How hard is her fate! But how great is her merit,
If by taking my all, she effects her release!

~ or ~

You may lie on my first by the side of a stream,
And my second compose to the nymph you adore,
But if, when you've none of my whole her esteem
And affection diminish – think of her no more!

Can you figure out the word for each? Need a little help? The answer to the first charade is *hemlock* and the answer to the second is *bank note*. Isn't that fun and how totally clever?! Jane Austen put her charade skills to use in *Emma* when Emma uses charades in the hopes of broadening Harriet's literary knowledge. She may not have had much luck in that endeavor but certainly succeeds in engaging Mr. Elton's unsolicited attention.

If cleverness of mind was not readily available in the

middle of a party, another popular game of longstanding was Snapdragon. This game called for raisins, brandy, nimbleness of fingers and plain old gumption. Raisins were placed in a shallow dish and then brandy poured over them. Once that's done, the brandy is set ablaze and lights in the room were extinguished so the eerie blue flame of the burning brandy could be seen more clearly. Each player was to demonstrate their courage by plucking

a raisin out of the flames and then eat the burning raisin at the risk of being burnt.

Samuel Johnson's *Dictionary of the English Language* (1755) described Snapdragon as "a play in which they catch raisins out of burning brandy and, extinguishing them by closing the mouth, eat them." Richard Steele's *Tatler* magazine contained an eighteenth-century article that stated, "the wantonness of the thing was to see each other look like a demon, as we burnt ourselves, and snatched out the fruit."

The game of Snapdragon even had its own song:

Here comes the flaming bowl,
Don't he mean to take his toll,
Snip! Snap! Dragon!
Take care you don't take too much,
Be not greedy in your clutch,
Snip! Snap! Dragon!

Balls to celebrate Twelfth Night could be held on either January 5th or 6th depending on the hostess' preference. The hostess who announced the date of her Ball first took precedence unless a hostess of greater consequence should announce a Ball for the same evening at a later date. Balls were the signature event but a

Parks' 12 Night Characters from 1843

masque ball in particular was a favorite for this holiday as it allowed participants to take part in the popular game of Twelfth Night Characters. This ancient game dates back hundreds of years to the time of the Romans when masters and servants switched places for the day.

In Regency England, the evening followed a traditional regimen. Celebrants arriving at the Ball would draw a card from a box held by a footman standing at the door. Ladies drew a card from a box held by the footman on the left while men drew a card from the box held by the footman on the right. The wealthy hired stationers to create unique sheets of cards for the evening that could not be duplicated for other parties. For the less wealthy, cheaper sets were available but were not exclusive. Not to worry though, stationers kept ledgers recording who bought which set so there would be no duplicates and thus prevent embarrassment of the hostess.

Each card was a caricatures of pairs and the character drawn had to be portrayed through the evening. As cards were drawn in pairs, each person was to find the compliment to their card's character including the King and Queen who ruled festivities for the evening. The search began with everyone acting out their character and depending on the liveliness of the party or the amount of spirits being enjoyed, the characters might become quite animated during the frivolities. The playacting was taken quite seriously too, for if someone broke character, a forfeit would have to be paid.

As one of Jane Austen's nieces wrote about a very festive Twelfth Night in 1806, "On Twelfth Day we were all agreeably surprised with a sort of masquerade, on being dressed into character, and then we were conducted into the library, which was all lighted up and at one end a throne, surrounded by a grove of Orange Trees and other shrubs, and all this was totally unknown to us all! Was it not delightful? . . . Edward and I were the Shepherd King and Queen, Mama a Savoyarde with a Hurdy-Gurdy . . . Uncle John– a Turk; Elizabeth a flowergirl . . . George– Harlequin; Henry– Clown; and Charley a Cupid! . . . Besides these great days we had Snapdragon, Bullet Pudding, and Apple in Water, as usual."

While these festivities and social events were in full swing, holiday foods were prepared to be enjoyed by the merrymakers. One of the foods especially significant to Twelfth Night was mincemeat pie. Fillings for mincemeat pies varied from region to region but pies generally might contain beef, spices, fowl, eggs, orange peel, apples,

brandy or even goose tongue. These pies were also known as Twelfth Night pies since they were made from leftovers from the Christmas Day feast. Mincemeat pie, traditionally, was to be eaten on each of the twelve days between Christmas Day and Epiphany to invite happiness and good luck into your home for the upcoming twelve months. To strengthen the charm, pies were to be baked by the dozen and offered by friends.

Have you noticed how the number 12 keeps popping up? 12 days between Christmas Day and Epiphany, mincemeat pies were to be baked by the dozen and eaten on each of those twelve days which was supposed to bring happiness in the next 12 months. This recurring number was no accident. Use of the number 12 during the holiday season was meant to reflect the importance of the number 12 in the Bible: 12 tribes of Israel, 12 apostles, the first significant recorded event in the life of Christ came at the age of 12, and symbolically, the number 12 represents God's working with man, etc.

The climax of the Twelfth Night ball was the cutting of the Twelfth Night cake which was the centerpiece of the party. The cake was quite large and its texture was much like a fruit cake. It was elaborately decorated with sugar frosting, gilded paper trimmings including two crowns for the king and queen of the evening and possibly, even little sugar paste figures. These cakes were creations of skilled confectioners who would proudly display them in their shop windows. So the cakes could be admired even at night in the local village, bakery windows were lit with small lamps.

Once the cake was cut, Twelfth Night festivities began to wind down for another year. Greenery was taken down and burned in the fireplace but this came with a word of caution to the wise. If all of the greenery wasn't burned by midnight on January 6th, the household could face bad luck in the coming year. Some even believed that for every piece of greenery left unburned after midnight, a goblin would appear!

The Yule log was extinguished and splinters were carefully saved to be used to light next year's log. The log's ashes were saved to spread over the fields to promote fertility for the next growing season.

The charming quaintness of a Regency Christmas appeals to all the good things found in a simpler time. Whether it was gathering around a Yuletide fire, sipping a cup of wassail, taking your turn stirring up the Christmas pudding, acting out a character on Twelfth Night or preparing a box full of goods for the poor, the emphasis was on spending time together and giving to or doing something for those less fortunate. There was a lot to celebrate at Epiphany and as its festivities came to an end, it was also the official end of the Christmastide season and the end of the full winter festival season which had started on All Hallow's Eve in October. As the joyous season drew to a close, family and friends happily returned home having received the best gift of all, time well spent with family and friends.

And in Conclusion . . .

A Journey Well Spent

"I expect a severe March, a wet April & a sharp May. –
And with that prophecy, I must conclude."
Jane Austen in a letter to her sister, Cassandra ~ February 1807

W E DID IT! WE'VE made it through a year jam-packed with birthdays, weddings and a myriad of holidays from Valentine's Day and Lady's Day, to Michaelmas and Hallow's Eve to Christmas and Twelfth Night. How fascinating to discover the many holidays celebrated during the Regency Era and to realize just how much we have in common with the people who lived during that time.

Sometimes, in taking a look at the past, we only see cobwebs and dust and wonder how anything that happened "way back then" could possibly matter to us today. It matters because as we've made our journey, we've come to realize that the people who lived during the Regency Era are important to us today because, just like us, they were people too. They had birthdays. They fell in love, had sweethearts and got married. They harvested crops and watched the weather. They took trips and enjoyed sea

bathing. They took care of those less fortunate and looked forward to the start of a new year. And we, like our Regency Era counterparts, enjoy the opportunity to celebrate occasions special to us. Holidays serve as a common thread woven through the years and across continents and oceans to bind us all together. Holidays are what people do to recognize and acknowledge what they have in common. Whether it be a shared heritage from the past or a recognition of a religious observance, all holidays have an even deeper meaning. They are our connection to the past, the future and to each other.

And as always - *Happy Holidays!*

Acknowledgments

"Because you are my help, I sing in the shadow of your wings. My soul clings to you; your right hand upholds me." Psalm 63:7-8

HOW DO I EVEN begin to thank the many people who have made such an impact on my life and whose help and encouragement made a dream become reality? The best place to start is at the beginning of course and that would absolutely have to be my parents, Leyton and Jonnie Bell. Thank you, Mom and Dad for all those little pushes that kept me going and for being the sounding board I so often needed. You inspired, encouraged and kept me moving forward. You guys are the best. I love you and thank you!

Special thanks to my incredible friend, Ann Gray. Ann kept me motivated - she is an amazing cheerleader. She believed in me and kept me believing I could do it. Ann is a great proof reader too so thank you, Ann, for unselfishly sharing your time and expertise but most importantly, thank you for being my friend. Betty Wiesepape, thank you for generously sharing your time to read the manuscript and for your valuable constructive comments. Your advice and insight into the world of publishing and authorship fell on fertile ground. I've planted the seeds of your wise words and feel better prepared to enter the

world of published authorship. A great big thank you to the many friends and co-workers who have shared in my excitement. Your enthusiasm and support have been both humbling and uplifting.

To those awesome PAT-1 authors – you know who you are – we've shared and continue to share an amazing adventure in this world called writing. The stimulating time we spent learning together provided the catalyst to complete this book and inspires me to continue writing. I'll never forget that weekend at Zermatt. Because of it, I can now say I am an author. Keep writing, my friends!

Dayna Linton, where would I be without your help, expertise and support? It is an absolute joy and pleasure to work with you in making this long-held dream a reality. Thank you. Thank you.

And to Richard Paul Evans, thank you for the opportunity to actually sit at your feet, to learn and be encouraged. You have inspired me for over 20 years through your books and now I have the good fortune of being able to call you mentor. You gave me the tools and knowledge to move confidently forward. You have my sincerest, warmest thanks.

To my friends in the Jane Austen Society of North America (especially the North Texas Region), you continue to inspire me with all there is to learn about the genius of Jane Austen. Thank you for providing the impetus and opportunity to continue learning so many remarkable things about this amazing author and which provided this occasion to share even a small portion of her world.

And to my family – thank you! Thanks to each and

every one of you for your support, enthusiasm, interest and untiring confidence. The reality of this book wouldn't mean as much without sharing the journey with each of you along the way. I love you!

Selected Bibliography

1. Addicted to Austen Blog Spot. Halloween Traditions of Regency England. http://addictedtoausten.blogspot.com/2012/10/halloween-traditions-of-regency-england.html.

2. Author Unknown. Candlemas. TimeandDate. www.timeanddate.com/holidays/common/candlemas.

3. Author Unknown. Easter Celebrations in the UK. https://www.learnenglish.de/culture/easter.html.

4. Author Unknown. The Goddess Brigid, Groundhog Day and a Message of Hope. http://www.goddessgift.com/Goddess_Path/Feb05.html. Reprinted from the Goddess Gift Newsletter, January 12, 2017.

5. Author Unknown. Halloween in the Regency. https://regencyredingote.wordpress.com/2014/10/31/halloween-in-the-regency/

6. Author Unknown. The History of Halloween. http://www.learnenglish.de/culture/halloween.html#sthash.KbDFwrid.dpuf

7. Author Unknown. The Importance of Lady Day in Regency England and in Wishing Game. www.writerspace.com/the-importance-of-lady-day-in-regency-england-and-in-wishing-game/.

8. Author Unknown. Maundy Thursday (Holy Thursday). www.projectbritain.com/easter/maundythursday.

9. Author Unknown. May Day - History and Origin. http://www.theholidayspot.com/mayday/history.htm#HGi58EywAJ8tajYB.99.

10. Author Unknown. Michaelmas Day. http://projectbritain.com/calendar/September/Michaelmas.html.

11. Author Unknown. Mothering Sunday in the United Kingdom. TimeandDate. www.timeanddate.com/holidays/uk/mothering-sunday.

12. Boyle, Laura. Advent of the Christmas Season. https://www.janeausten.co.uk/the-advent-of-the-christmas-season/

13. Boyle, Laura. All Hallow's Eve. https://www.janeausten.co.uk/author/laura-sauer/page/87/?add-to-cart=48664

14. Boyle, Laura. Christmas Charades and Bullet Pudding. https://www.janeausten.co.uk/christmas-charades-and-bullet-pudding/

15. Boyle, Laura. Hot Cross Buns. https://www.janeausten.co.uk/hot-cross-buns/

16. Boyle, Laura. Twelfth Night. https://www.janeausten.co.uk/twelfth-night/.

17. Boyle, Laura. Weddings During the Regency Era. https://www.janeausten.co.uk/weddings-during-the-regency-era/

18. Brighton & Hove Museums. Discover the Royal Pavilion. http://www.victoriana.com/Travel/royalpavilion.html

19. Burkhard, Lenore Rose. Carlton House, Celebrating the Season in Regency Style.

20. Dawson, William Francis. Christmas: It's Originations and Associations. https://janeaustensworld.wordpress.com/2007/12/24/christmas-traditions-from-the-regency-era/.

21. DeVito, Carl. Jane Austen Christmas – Celebrating the Season of Romance, Ribbons & Mistletoe. Kennebunkport, ME. Cider Mill Press. 2015.

22. Donnelly, Shannon – The Regency Holiday Season. https://shannondonnelly.com/2015/11/08/regency-holiday-traditions/

23. Emick, Jennifer, February 2, Candlemas, Imbolc, Feast of Purification. www.northernway.org/school/way/calendar/candlemas.html.

24. Grace, Maria. A Regency Holiday Calendar. http://englishhistoryauthors.blogspot.com/2013/11/a-regency-holiday-calendar.html.

25. Greenspan, Jesse. Guy Fawkes Day, A Brief History. http://www.history.com/news/guy-fawkes-day-a-brief-history.

26. History.com Staff. April Fools Tradition Popularized. www.history.com/this-day-in-history/april-fools-tradition-popularized.

27. Housman, A.E. The Lent Lily.

28. Jeffers, Regina. Celebrating Boxing Day. https://reginajeffers.blog/2014/12/26/celebrating-boxing-day-2/

29. Johnson, Ben. Michaelmas. http://www.historic-uk.com/CultureUK/Michaelmas/

30. Johnson, Ben. St. George – Patron Saint of England. http://www.historic-uk.com/HistoryUK/HistoryofEngland/St-George-Patron-Saint-of-England/

31. Johnson, Samuel. Dictionary of the English Language (1755)

32. Jones, Hunter S. Midsummer Magic in Tudor England. http://englishhistoryauthors.blogspot.com/2015/06/midsummer-magic-in-tudor-england.html.

33. Kane, Kathryn. The Importance of Lady Day in the Regency Calendar. https://regencyredingote.wordpress.com/2010/09/03/the-importance-of-lady-day-in-the-regency-calendar/

34. Knowles, Rachel. The Prince Regent's Fete. http://www.regencyhistory.net/2012/06/prince-regents-fete.html

35. Lathan, Sharon. All Saints/All Souls Day. http://sharonlathanauthor.com/all-saints-all-souls-days/

36. Lathan, Sharon. The Legalities. http://sharonlathanauthor.com/regency-marriage-the-legalities/

37. Lathan, Sharon. Saint Valentine and Valentine's Day. https://sharonlathanauthor.com/valentine-day-origins/

38. Lathan, Sharon – Today is Epiphany Day. http://sharonlathanauthor.com/january-6-is-epiphany-day/

39. Le Faye, Dierdre. Jane Austen's Letters (4th Edition). New York. Oxford University Press. 2011.

40. Mayer, Nancy. Christmas Pantomimes History. http://www.susannaives.com/nancyregencyresearcher/

41. Mikkelson, Davis. Boxing Day. http://www.snopes.com/holidays/christmas/boxingday.asp

42. Nokes, David. Jane Austen: A Life. USA. University of California Press. 1998

43. Rosin, Nancy. Nancy's Puzzle Purse Valentine. http://www.victoriantreasury.com/library/2007-01_Puzzle_Purses/

44. Seasonal Wisdom. Historical Look at May Day. http://www.seasonalwisdom.com/2009/05/a-historical-look-at-may-day/

45. Thackeray, William Makepeace. Round About the Christmas Tree.

46. Thiselton-Dyer, Thomas Firminger. British Popular Customs. London, England. George Bell & Sons. 1876.

47. Tribe, Shawn. Customs of Martinmas and the Feast of St. Martin of Tours. http://www.newliturgicalmovement.org/2009/11/customs-of-martinmas-feast-of-st-martin.html#.Way4iMh942w.

48. Vic. Wassailing. https://janeaustensworld.wordpress.com/2007/12/01/the-wassailing-of-trees/

49. Walker, Regan. Christmas Traditions in Regency England. http://thewritewaycafe.blogspot.com/2014/12/christmas-traditions-in-regency-england.html#.Way94sh942w.

50. Waugh, Joanna. Christmas Feast. http://joannawaugh.blogspot.com/2008/12/christmas-feast.html

51. Zaterdag. During, Jane Austen's Day, the Easter Season. http://kleurrijkjaneausten.blogspot.com/2014/04/during-jane-austens-day-easter-season.html.

About the Author

LINDY DEVELOPED AN INTEREST in Jane Austen and all things related to her genteel world a few short years ago and that interest soon blossomed into love. That love has spilled over into various Regency Era-related topics including the research of holidays of the era, their origins, how they were celebrated and how they appear in Jane Austen's novels and personal letters. A member of the Jane Austen Society of North America, Lindy has spoken to a variety of groups and has taught Continuing and Adult Professional Education classes on Regency Era holidays at Southern Methodist University (SMU).

A graduate of Abilene Christian University, Lindy lives in Plano, Texas and works for an area convention and visitors bureau assisting visitors to and residents of the Dallas/Fort Worth Metroplex. As hobbies, Lindy enjoys writing, reading an engaging novel or cross stitching delicate patterns – Jane Austen-related (of course) and otherwise.

Jane Austen Celebrates is Lindy's first book with a second book, a novel, currently in the works.

Find Lindy On Social Media

WEBSITE:

LindyBellWrites.com

FACEBOOK:

www.facebookcom/LindyBellWrites/

TWITTER:

@LindyBellWrites

INSTAGRAM:

LindyBellWrites

PINTEREST:

Lindy Bell Writes - Regency Holidays